D1042154

*Praise for*
# A Very Fine House

Barbara Stoefen is a member of the club that none of us ever hoped to belong to, and I'm glad she turned her lessons into helping tools for the rest of us. As the mother of a recovering addict myself, I found myself relating strongly to Barbara's journey. And she also offered clear information on addiction that gave me new insights, as well as hope for the future. A mother's prayers do make a difference.

> TERRI BLACKSTOCK, author of *Intervention*, *Vicious Cycle*, and *Downfall*

Having read many memoirs about addiction, this is the possibly one of the finest. Ms. Stoefen beautifully writes her story of facing the stinging truth of a child's addiction and, eventually, the sublime struggle to build a life in recovery. If I could, I'd put this book into the hands of every parent in need of hope.

> DEBRA JAY, author of *It Takes a Family: A Cooperative Approach to Lasting Sobriety*

Wow. *A Very Fine House* is a very fine book indeed—and long overdue in our marketplace. Barbara Stoefen's heart-wrenching story about dealing with her daughter's addiction will keep readers turning pages. Her hard-won wisdom will help parents of addicts feel less alone and, more importantly, respond to their child's addiction in ways that will save lives. Every person who loves an addict or parents teens should read this book.

> HEATHER KOPP, author of *Sober Mercies: How Love Caught Up with a Christian Drunk*

*A Very Fine House* truly captures the portrait of addiction. Barbara Stoefen describes clearly and movingly the arc of the disease —how an otherwise affable, capable, lovable young person can become irrational and unrecognizable. I found it remarkable how closely her words fit what is known about the neuroscience of addiction.

But what makes *A Very Fine House* so enjoyable and so important is that Barbara doesn't just describe how the brain shuts down and the dreadful behaviors that result; she describes something far more wondrous: how the brain comes back on, and how heartbreak and anger can turn into healing and joy. Hers is a voice that parents will not only recognize but need to hear so they, too, can begin the journey from common tragedy to shared triumph.

KEVIN MCCAULEY, MD, founder of Institute for Addiction Study

Barbara Stoefen's *A Very Fine House* is truly a gift: the story of a mother's fierce love, a daughter's descent into the darkness of addiction, and a life-changing journey of recovery. Barb's book is a compelling read—written courageously and candidly, engaging the reader in every chapter with her unique and vulnerable style. I'm already recommending it to people I know.

CHERI FULLER, speaker and author of *Mother-Daughter Duet* and *When Mothers Pray*

# A Very Fine House

# A Very Fine House

## A Mother's Story of
## Love, Faith, and Crystal Meth

## Barbara Cofer Stoefen

ZONDERVAN

*A Very Fine House*
Copyright © 2014 by Barbara Cofer Stoefen

This title is also available as a Zondervan ebook. Visit www.zondervan.com/ebooks.

Requests for information should be addressed to:

Zondervan, 3900 *Sparks Dr. SE, Grand Rapids, Michigan 49546*

Library of Congress Cataloging-in-Publication Data

Stoefen, Barbara Cofer, 1953–
    A very fine house : a mother's story of love, faith, and crystal meth / Barbara
Cofer Stoefen.
       pages cm
    ISBN 978-0-310-34441-4 (hardcover)
    1. Stoefen, Barbara Cofer, 1953– 2. Parents of drug addicts—United States
—Biography. 3. Drug addicts—Rehabilitation—United States. 4. Mothers and
daughters—United States. 5. Christian life—United States. I. Title.
HV5805.S76A3 2014
362.29'953092—dc23
   [B]                                      2014010095

Published in association with the literary agency of WordServe Literary Group, Ltd.,
(www.wordserveliterary.com).

*Cover design: Faceout Studio*
*Cover photography: Shutterstock®*
*Interior photography: Shutterstock®*
*Interior design: Beth Shagene*

*First Printing July 2014 / Printed in the United States of America*

*To Annie,*
*who has taught me more about love and life*
*than I ever wanted to learn,*
*and to Jeff,*
*who gave me great hope for the future*

⇀•↽

# Contents

# PART THREE

# Author's Note

If you've picked up this book, it's likely because you love an addict. You're undoubtedly suffering—I know because I've been there. I've felt your despair, your feelings of helplessness and hopelessness, the grief we all fear.

Several excellent books have been written by parents who have chronicled their journey through a child's addiction, and I recommend them all. By adding my story to the others, I hope to share not just what happened but also what I learned and what helped me to cope and to see my way to safety.

Many friends have referred their friends and relatives to me, people who seek some nugget of wisdom for their own journey. I hope that by writing my story, I can be a validating voice to your experience, possibly even giving you permission to think and say things you may not yet have dared to acknowledge.

I also want to offer you hope that recovery is indeed possible, not only for your loved one, but for yourself as well. Addiction in the family will change you. You can allow the change to consume and damage you, or you can embrace the lessons that life now presents. Perhaps you will not just survive but actually flourish— and hopefully forgive.

I am sharing our story with my daughter's permission and

blessing. Everything I've written is true, including the dialogue, which is accurate to the best of my recollection. For the ease of storytelling, a few scenes are composites of more than one event. The names and details of many of the individuals depicted have been changed to protect anonymity, but some are real and have been included with permission.

. . .

I've heard it said that in every problem there is a gift. The many gifts I received along the way have helped carry and sustain me. I now share these gifts with you.

# Too Late

I couldn't shake the sense of foreboding I felt upon waking that Easter Sunday morning. As on most April days in our mountain community, I could see my breath in the early morning air as I stood at the back door and called Delores, our yapping pointer-heeler, back into the house. She'd surprised three mule deer that had camped under a large ponderosa for the night, and the resulting ruckus pierced the calm of the new day.

From the door I scanned the yard's open landscape and marveled at the patches of snow that still clung to the northern fringes of our treed property. There was no hint of spring. I savored the traces of wood smoke that wafted through the high branches and realized our neighbors were rising as well. While this same scene had stirred my love for Oregon and its peaceful vistas countless times before, the still-barren bitterbrush and lifeless sage mirrored my sunken mood.

Our entire extended family planned to gather in a couple of hours for brunch at the home of my husband's sister and brother-in-law. Robin and Gary had followed us to Bend a few years before and found their dream house just three doors down. Our family congregated for most holidays, though we were few enough now to fit comfortably inside a Suburban. With all four grandparents gone, it was just Pete and me and our two children, Annie and Jeff, plus Robin and Gary and my brother, Paul, the last California holdout who'd just moved to Portland.

I was particularly eager to see my daughter that day. Jeff was a high school junior and still at home, but Annie was twenty-one. We'd recently moved her into an apartment a few miles away. With nearly three years of college behind her but no plans to continue, Annie's life had been a series of fits and starts that had taken a toll on our relationship. The two of us rarely had time together anymore. In fact, I wasn't even certain she'd show up for brunch that day.

Easter was no longer the event it had been when the kids were little. Back then, Pete and I rose at dawn to hide candy and decorated eggs throughout our secluded front yard. A massive volcanic berm formed a natural privacy screen, and the trees and dense brush that covered it provided endless hiding places. It was a painful excursion in biting cold that required hats and gloves and parkas over our pj's, yet the reward of watching the kids' determined hunt made it worthwhile.

I well remember one of those mornings. After I rallied them from sleep, Annie and Jeff charged out the front door in their Lands' End long-john pajamas, Annie in red-and-pink stripes and Jeff in green-and-blue. Each with a basket in tow, they took off in opposite directions down the deep circular driveway that wrapped around the berm. Annie's long brown hair flew behind her as she ran, and Jeff's towheaded mop bounced as he stooped to capture each hidden treasure. Five years his senior and a head taller, Annie dominated the hunt. But when she deemed her basket full enough, she ultimately took pity on her little brother and helped him find the last few eggs.

"Over here, Jeffy!" she called. Grateful to be wherever his sister was, he obediently came running, wearing the satisfied smile of one who'd just been picked for the cool team. "See, there are tons of eggs left. You can have all of these, Jeff."

Once back in the house, the kids assessed their brimming baskets, divvied up the Peeps, fought over the Reese's eggs, and bit the ears off their chocolate bunnies. Given the early hour and predictable sugar crash, Annie and Jeff both inevitably collapsed in tears over some perceived slight. But all was soon forgotten.

After gulping a quick breakfast, the four of us then got ready for church. I loved helping Annie dress for Easter — and for all special occasions. I took a mental photograph of nearly every dress she wore. I probably made half of them. Once dressed, we stood together in front of the bathroom mirror, where I meticulously curled the ends of her hair. We kept a bin in her bedroom with satin and grosgrain ribbons in every width and color, so the perfect finishing touch was always readily at hand.

Now that the kids were older, I longed to revisit those innocent years. When Annie did arrive at Robin and Gary's that Easter, even almost on time, I had her in my arms before she crossed the threshold.

"Annie, you're *here*. I'm so happy to see you." Jealous over the thought that her dad or brother might get their hands on her first, I ferried her into the kitchen.

Annie wore cream-colored slacks and a flattering pale-pink, cowl-necked sweater. Looking especially tall in heels beneath her already extra-long inseam, and with her sun-streaked locks ironed to perfection, she was stunning. People always noticed Annie's good looks. While I also enjoyed her beauty, it bugged me that her appearance was what people seemed to appreciate most about her. She was so much more than a pretty face. Annie was bright and intense — so talented, creative, and *fun*. I'd always laughed more with Annie than anyone. She was drawn to people who rated highly on her fun-o-meter and had never been particularly impressed by wealth or materialism. I liked that about her. She'd take a friend who could blow bubbles out of her nose any day over someone who slung a boring designer bag over a suntanned shoulder.

"You look lovely," I said, "but what's with the sunglasses? It's so dreary out today. I'm surprised you can even see in those things."

"Oh, I woke up with kind of a headache and just want to keep the glare down. I'll take 'em off later. No big deal."

My mom antenna shot up. "Um ... okay. Are you all right?"

"Yeah, I'm just tired, and my head hurts. But look at this." Annie lifted her sweater to show off her smaller middle, obviously proud of the weight she'd just lost.

"Look at you, skinny minnie. Wow. Guess we need to feed you today." I couldn't remember when I'd seen Annie so thin. It unsettled me. But exhausted by my incessant fretting over her in recent months, and craving a return to normality, I dismissed my concern as needless worry. I was just so happy to see my daughter. While the family talked Giants baseball in the living room, a holdover from our California days, Annie and I remained in the kitchen, warming rolls in the oven and filling water glasses for the table.

"So how's it going with the new apartment?" I asked.

"It's good. I like it. I still can't afford a couch, but that futon you gave me works great. Oh, and I put those colored vases that were Nan's on the windowsill over the sink."

"Your grandma loved you so much, Annie. I'm glad you have those vases to remind you of her. I still can't believe she's gone." I missed my mother but shook off the sadness. "Say, is that plant we found for that one corner in your living room still alive?"

"Uh, well, it's technically still alive, but watering it would probably help."

We both laughed and carried the last of the water glasses to the table.

"I miss you," I said. "When can we have a date? It's been eons since we've seen a movie together. You up for something next week?"

Annie looked away. "Uh, can I let you know? I'm not sure about my hours at the store, and I've just been really busy lately."

My heart sank at Annie's obvious disinterest. "Sure, just give me a holler when you can. How do you like the new job?"

"It's okay," she said with a sigh. "Selling office supplies isn't exactly my idea of nirvana, but it'll do for now. I must say the crew's a pretty wild bunch."

"Wild fun or wild bad?"

"We'll see," she said.

"Any thoughts of finishing school? If you finished up your science degree at the college, you could ..."

"Mom, stop." There was an edge to her tone. "Can we not talk about school? I'm just so sick of it. It wasn't getting me anywhere anyway."

"Okay, I'm sorry. It just seems a shame, since you're so close to finishing."

Annie often silenced me these days. It had me tiptoeing around her. We'd been so close during her growing-up years, and she'd shared so much of her life with me. In the past year, though, I'd felt so ... incidental. There wasn't anything I had that she seemed to want anymore.

Those few precious moments together in the kitchen, so much like the old days, now seemed spoiled. I was relieved when Robin called us to the dining room to eat.

• • •

After brunch, the family headed back to the living room, this time with Jeff leading a discussion about the NFL Draft. Annie helped me clear the table. I was glad to have another chance to reconnect with her privately in the kitchen. Her sunglasses were now off, and while she looked exhausted, the mood had lightened again, and we were back to girl talk.

She gushed once more about her weight loss and gave her flat belly a satisfying pat.

"How are you losing so much weight?" I asked.

"Just not eating much. Food doesn't really appeal to me right now, I guess."

I pressed further, wanting to know if she was taking care of herself. Every time Annie moved out, she had difficulty managing things on her own. Without the structure of the home life we'd always provided, she became easily overwhelmed. There had been too much partying at school and battles with depression. I *always* worried about that.

"I'm fine, Mom. Don't worry—I know what I'm doing."

*I know what I'm doing?* Her comment seemed to imply something surreptitious. The uneasiness I'd felt over the sunglasses and her surly mood returned. Something was up.

Always the helicopter mom, I wanted to fix whatever was amiss in Annie's life. I figured if you were careful enough, you could protect your child from anything and everything. I embraced the classic mother's mantras: Eat your vegetables; get a good night's sleep; don't forget your coat; lock the door; fasten your seat belt; look both ways; watch out for ice; watch out for deer; slow down; be careful; just say no; don't ride with people you don't know; call me; be home by midnight; don't drink, but if you do, don't drive—call us and we'll come get you, no questions asked; and don't do drugs—they're bad.

I'd actually made a mental note earlier that week to talk with both Annie and Jeff about all the recent press in our town regarding meth. I thought myself pretty hip, but I really didn't know much about it. It wasn't something we talked about when I was coming of age in the early '70s. I figured I should add it to the litany of warnings I regularly issued my kids, in spite of the abuse I always suffered for doing so. From what I'd read, methamphetamine was like cocaine on steroids, and the long-term physical and psychological effects were devastating. The scariest thing of all was that meth virtually hijacked the brain. It was nearly impossible to quit.

I had never really worried about Annie and drugs, although I knew she'd smoked some pot while away at school. She'd always been terrified of most drugs and looked down on the people who used them. I took comfort in that. She did drink entirely too much alcohol, though.

"You're not doing anything dumb to lose this weight, are you?" I asked. "You wouldn't take diet pills, would you?"

"No, Mom, I'm not taking diet pills," she answered. Annie tolerated my questioning, so I kept going.

"You're not purging, are you?"

"No — eeww, no! I love being skinnier, but I really haven't been trying to lose weight. Quit worrying."

"I know," I said. "I'm a worrier. No need for anyone else to spend their time worrying, because I do such a good job of it for all of us. But since we're on the subject of worry, I do need to warn you about something. Have you been hearing any of the talk about that meth drug? I know you're way too smart to get mixed up with anything like that, but the new crowd you're working with might not be. Whatever you do, steer clear of that stuff. It's like the worst drug ever. I hear there's no coming back from it."

I waited for Annie's trademark insulted response, with the classic eye roll and the defensive line, *Do you think I'm stupid?* Instead, she looked straight into my eyes and answered in an almost whimsical tone.

"Too late."

Silence filled the room.

It's hard to describe how I felt at that moment because I'd never experienced anything like that before — or since. As I heard those two words and took in the depth of their meaning, time stood still. A warm flush of terror slowly cascaded from the crown of my head down the back of my neck and onto my shoulders and arms, coming to rest as a swirling eddy inside my core. In that instant, in a deep and profound way, life changed forever.

# PART ONE

*If I could live forever— and you could be with me . . .*
*I'd choose a house for all seasons in a mountain greenery.*

D. MORGAN

❧ • ☙

# CHAPTER 1

# The Oregon Trail

"Eeeeeeeeeeeeeee ... yeowwwww!"

Annie's shrieks brought me flying from the back of the house. I found my ten-year-old daughter sprawled on the tile floor at the foot of the stairs, cocooned inside a shiny green nylon sleeping bag. She was moving, so I guessed she wasn't dead. I peeled back a corner of the bag and found her red-faced and heaving with silent belly laughs.

No sooner did I reach the scene than her little brother, wrapped inside his own sleeping bag, barreled into her back. Seems the two of them had just tobogganed down the stairs. Both wore the flushed excitement of a child exiting an eTicket ride at Disneyland.

"Let's go again, Jeffy!" Annie was already scrambling back to the top of the stairs.

"Wait a second, you two," I said. "Pete! I thought you were watching them. Do you even know what the kids are doing?"

My husband peeked around the corner from the kitchen, grinning. "Relax, Barb," he said. "I haven't seen any blood yet. They're fine."

"This can't be safe," I said.

"I think it's fine. I told 'em they couldn't go down headfirst."

"Watch this, Mom!" Annie yelled from above. This time, she and Jeff careened down in tandem. "Huh-huh-huh-huh-huh ... hahahahhahahahaha. Owwwweeee ... Mommm." When their heads collided at the foot of the stairs, Annie's distress amplified throughout the house, while Jeff remained merely stunned.

That was my girl. She was quick to collapse into animated laughter at the slightest instigation, but also just as easily moved to tears.

• • •

Three years earlier, Pete and I had moved our young family from California to Bend, Oregon. We had discovered it as newlyweds on a Northwest road trip, and after carrying a torch for years for the little town with a river running through it, we finally acted on our passion.

I found our house during a mini vacation when I'd recruited my mom, brother, and Annie to take a train trip with me up to Oregon. Pete couldn't miss work, so he stayed behind, and two-year-old Jeff kept his schedule at day care.

I had endured a terrible postpartum depression following Jeff's birth, even more profound than the depression that had dogged me after Annie was born. When I'd returned to work after maternity leave and once again put on that coat of corporate responsibility, the coat no longer seemed to fit. It just hung on me as if I'd been out in the rain for too long. I couldn't muster the energy to even pretend I cared about that world anymore. I needed a change. I craved greater authenticity and reinvention, not to mention a saner pairing of work life and motherhood. So when the four of us weren't romping in Bend's fresh dump of February snow, we looked at real estate. After two days on the housing trail, I called Pete from our hotel to pose a provocative question.

"Honey, do you still, uh, maybe want to move to Oregon? I just made an offer on a house ..."

Pete agreed to the purchase, sight unseen. Within ninety days we sold our home in Saratoga, California, quit our management jobs at Silicon Valley tech companies, and pulled the kids out of school and day care. Our family made our way north in a Volvo station wagon. It wasn't exactly the Oregon Trail, but Pete still hadn't seen the house, and we had no idea how we were going to make a living.

Our new home was a big house on a couple of acres just outside the city limits. We lived with fifty towering ponderosas, scores of chipmunks and quail that darted in and out of manzanita bushes, and an owl that sometimes posed as a cat, sitting regally on the asphalt at the end of our driveway. The neighborhood was also home to herds of mule deer, as well as screaming coyotes that celebrated catching their prey not far from our open windows at night.

The first painting tacked on the walls of our new home was a watercolor I gave to Pete on our seventh wedding anniversary. It depicted a country house by a river, surrounded by tall pines. How fitting it was that we were now living that dream. It thrilled me to write "Bend" in the return address of our outgoing mail.

A peek through the window from the wraparound porch of our home would have revealed a Norman Rockwellesque existence, a classic American life resplendent with all the trimmings and bubbling sentiment. Mom and dad, boy and girl, dog and cats, a bountiful table, and the glow of a crackling fire behind a large brick hearth. I was framed inside the painting of my dreams, and it was wonderful to be me.

Those first years in Bend were wonderful for Annie too. Each day she'd get off the school bus at the top of our long driveway and skip toward the house, swinging her long, skinny arms and legs in perfect unison.

"How was your day?" I'd ask as she bounded through the front door.

"Oh, fine," was her usual winded, singsong response. She'd stoop to ruffle the coat of her puppy, a golden retriever she'd named Cindy after one of her stuffed animals. She'd then collect her black cat in her arms and be out the door again, dashing through the brush to the neighbor girl's house. Without a care in the world, my second grader was a picture of complete and utter contentment.

Annie enjoyed a small group of close friends; Brownies, then Girl Scouts; modern dance and ballet; and Sunday school. She loved to draw and paint, and she drew countless pictures of Jesus on the cross, paying particular attention to the tiny details of his splattered blood and tears.

She built forts in her bedroom and the yard, entertained her little brother with dress-up and puppetry, and beat everyone, young or old, at any game requiring memorization. Annie was wickedly bright.

"Oh, that's simple," she'd say as she rattled off the names of all fifty states in alphabetical order. With a talking globe her favorite toy, Annie knew where Chad was located, and Kyrgyzstan too. She could spell the former but not the latter. While she never won a spelling contest, she did excel at many things.

Preferring puzzles and word games over baby dolls and Barbies, Annie was feminine but not a girlie girl. She played well with most of the neighborhood kids and those at school. Fun-loving and precocious, Annie was mostly obedient. She was also, however, strong willed. She wanted what she wanted when she wanted it.

"Anna is disruptive in class," her teacher reported at the second grade parent-teacher conference. She used Annie's formal, given name, which seemed foreign to me at the time. "I've given her an 'office' of her own in the back of the classroom."

This puzzled me—when I was growing up, it was the rough-and-tumble boys who acted out in class, not the little girls. At a loss to understand Annie's behavior, I asked the teacher if she thought it possible that Annie might need more challenging work. The teacher's reply was laced with indignation.

"If you're suggesting that Anna is too advanced for what we're doing in class, I can assure you that is *not* the case."

I wasn't suggesting anything. My daughter hadn't come with

an instruction manual, and I was just trying to figure her out. She was typically a pleasure at home, and I had no idea how to account for her acting out in class.

Toward the end of that school year, Annie tested in the top 1 percent on national standardized tests, and at age seven she was reported to be reading at the seventh-grade level. Maybe she was bored after all. Annie was then identified for the school district's Talented and Gifted program, but there was little vindication. Unlike the other TAG students, Annie didn't engage. She sometimes appeared lazy, and when she did complete an assignment, she couldn't always be counted on to turn it in.

"I forgot," she whined. "Why does it matter anyway? Isn't the important thing that I did it?"

While there might have been some validity to her argument from a learning standpoint, I assured Annie that wouldn't cut it in the real world. Someday she'd have a landlord who would demand that the rent check make it from Annie's purse into his pocket.

Annie also lost clothes. Any removable article of clothing invariably went missing, either on the playground, the school bus, or whatever vortex it is where socks in the dryer also go missing. Her things simply disappeared without a trace.

Teachers didn't know what to make of this smart kid who couldn't, or wouldn't, keep track of her things or consistently complete her work. We did our best at home to hold Annie accountable, but no enticements or chastisements, carrots or sticks, seemed to make much difference.

Pete and I couldn't decide if Annie was marching to the beat of a different drummer or if something else was holding her back. Maybe she just didn't care. Whatever the reason, "failure to work to your potential" was the resounding refrain Annie heard throughout her school years. She grew to hate the sound of it. By fifth grade, Annie was described to us by her teacher as "one of the top ten brightest students I've had in my twenty years of teaching." Yet he also described her as "flaky."

• • •

"He's gone?" Annie cried the following year. "No, Mom, no!"

"I'm so sorry, sweetie." I took Annie in my arms. "I know how much you loved your Bapa, and we will all miss him. But it was his time."

"It wasn't his time! I prayed and prayed. He wasn't supposed to die."

"God hears our prayers, Annie, but we don't always get what we ask for. And your grandfather was in his eighties. He'd had a good life."

"God is dumb. What good is praying anyway?"

Annie had just started middle school when my father-in-law, Art, was diagnosed with cancer. His death six months later came as a terrible blow. Pete's parents had followed us to Bend that first year, and living just a mile away, they'd been a huge part of our lives.

"Bapa, watch me!" Annie sometimes hollered as she did cart-wheels across the back lawn.

"I see you, honey," he'd yell back to her. "Now c'mere and sit with your ol' grandpa. I'm all tuckered out from pushing you and your brother around in that wheelbarrow all afternoon." She'd then come running, plop onto his lap, and burrow in.

Art's passing was Annie's first experience with death. Her heart was completely broken, and she was plenty mad at God. She cried and cried, and when she was still crying months later, it became apparent that something was very wrong.

I knew enough about depression to recognize it in Annie because of my own experience in the months following her birth and Jeff's. While my depression had been hormonally induced, I knew traumatic life events could also trigger severe depression in those who are prone to it. Depression ran in Pete's family too, and its close cousin, anxiety, was the trademark affliction in my own family.

I didn't know that even children could become depressed.

While she wasn't deemed suicidal and had never constructed a plan to end her life, the therapist we found to treat her reported that Annie did have some suicidal thoughts. She was only eleven years old! How could such a bright and shiny child with a loving family and all that the world has to offer feel so hopeless?

"Make it go away, Mom," she said to me one night. "I can't stand how I feel." There was a physical restlessness in her body, and succumbing to sleep was difficult. It was just as hard to rouse her and get her moving in the mornings.

Over time, Annie's mental health did improve, though she was still easily overwhelmed. Her therapist told me her life would probably always look "messy."

"Annie is extremely sensitive. She lacks the protective exterior many of us have that helps deflect injury," I was told. "She's also extremely bright and special in the way she processes information. She's not a linear thinker like you are, Barb. She's creative to the nth degree."

What Annie went through terrified me. I was afraid to even look at it because of what I might see. Could she be one of those children who, well, just doesn't make it? I'd known some. I shudder at the memory and at the knowledge that my life would have been over had I lost her. I needed her to be okay so I, too, could be okay.

While I think most mothers are inherently codependent to at least some extent, a new attachment to my daughter was born that year. "I'll be strong for both of us," I told her. I was sure that if I stayed close enough and kept vigilant guard over Annie, I'd be able to protect her and fend off future trouble. I thought this was my job as her mother, and I would carry her through life until she could walk on her own.

Annie did begin to thrive again. She joined the jazz choir at school. Singing became her one true joy, the anchor that kept her grounded not only during the rest of middle school but also throughout her high school years.

The onset of adolescence was strangely elusive, though, and

Annie waited impatiently to catch up with her peers. Kids made cruel jokes about her still-juvenile appearance, and there were plenty of tears when she stood alone at school dances. She hated looking young.

When adolescence finally did hit, it exploded. There was always plenty of drama, and Annie kept us running just to keep up. First, there was the competitive love-hate relationship with her best girlfriend that exhausted everyone who came in the path of its fury. And when of age, there were boys. Lots of them. With her girl-next-door good looks and a stick figure that had yielded to curves, Annie had more guy friends than girlfriends.

The attention from boys, and the heady rush it delivered, became the tonic for my daughter's years of depression and low self-esteem. She was like a kid in a candy store, excited and wide-eyed. With plenty of currency at her disposal, she wanted to sample each flavor in every size and shape.

By the time Annie turned seventeen, she'd been dating "another one of those mouth breathers," as Pete liked to call him, for several months. He was a nice enough kid, I guess, and I especially liked the fact that he was active in a teenage movement about sexual abstinence. He even counseled younger teens about it. Their relationship ended abruptly, however, the summer before her senior year. Annie was devastated.

"Mom, I haven't heard from him in weeks. He told me he still wants to be friends. Do you think he'll even call me before he leaves for college?"

"I don't know," I told her. "I know this is painful, Annie, and I went through it too, but the truth is, most high school romances don't last. Try to find a place for him in your heart that doesn't hurt too much and just try to move on. I promise it will get easier. Just be glad it didn't get any more, well, serious than it did between you two."

"But it did—it did get serious. Mom ... we had ... sex." Annie had been sitting on the edge of her bed, and she collapsed into her pillow, sobbing. "And get this. He breaks up with me like a week later, telling me I'd *taken him away from God.* Do you believe that? Apparently I'm that powerful. And now all his friends hate me too."

I was shocked. Sleeping with her boyfriend did seem a mockery of the promise ring Pete and I had given her the year before. But I felt such compassion for Annie. The scene that played out before me was exactly the kind of pain I'd always wanted to protect her from.

Pete and I wanted to pummel the boyfriend—Pete for the sex, and me for the blame and shame he cast onto my daughter. He took no responsibility of his own, especially given that the "things he didn't want to do" were apparently done in his grandmother's bed.

It was the first time I'd seen my husband really cry.

The high school rumor mill was whirring, and Annie got the holier-than-thou cold shoulder from the boy's many friends. Their message came through loud and clear: *You're not good enough to be one of us.* It was bullying in the name of God.

"I always hate this time of year," she said when her senior year began, "when I have to start walking those halls again. It will be even worse now with everything that's happened."

The bumps of life seemed harder for Annie than they had been for me. Her distress always unsettled me. I had only one more year left to try to toughen her up.

# CHAPTER 2

# Hello, God?

"Hi, Barb; it's Zach. So ... um ... Anna isn't feeling very well right now, and she wanted me to call you. Is it okay if she stays here a little while longer?" It was just past midnight, and only the second time Annie had ever missed curfew.

"What's she doing at your house, Zach? I thought she was out with the girls tonight."

"She was, and then she came here."

"Can you please put Annie on the phone and let me talk with her?"

"Well, she's in the bathroom. She's not feeling very well."

"If she's not feeling well, she should be home." Annie had seemed fine earlier in the evening. I wondered if she was coming down with a bug. No sooner did that thought materialize, however, when the lightbulb in my head illuminated.

"Zach, has Annie been drinking?"

"Hold on a minute." I could hear whispering in the background, as if he was consulting Annie for permission to respond. Zach came back on the phone. "Yes. Yes, she has."

I shook my head and muffled a chuckle. I realize it sounds terribly unparental, but I found the clandestine exchange between Annie and her new boyfriend pretty amusing. With a visual of her curled around the toilet, it seemed my daughter had just experienced a rite of passage. Just a few months shy of eighteen and soon to head off to college, she must have decided it was time for a run-in with alcohol. Unlikely as it may seem in today's culture, it really was her first.

I forced a stern directive to Zach. "Bring Annie home right now. Oh, wait—have you been drinking too?"

"No, not at all. I wasn't out tonight. Cari brought her over here not long ago."

"Okay, good. Then please bring her home. I'll expect you in about ten minutes."

Pete was in bed asleep, so I perched myself on the back of the couch in the family room and waited. In the stillness of the room at that late hour, I yawned and marveled at our good fortune. While I wasn't wild about the stream of boyfriends that had come and gone throughout high school, I was grateful Annie had never caused us concern about alcohol and drugs. We were so lucky in that regard.

I'd done some drinking in high school, for sure. The first I remember was during a visit to see my older brother at college. I was a high school freshman, he a college freshman attending the University of California at Santa Cruz. It was just a thirty-minute hop over the small mountain range that separated our town of Saratoga from the coast, and Paul had invited me to spend the weekend. My first night there we stargazed in the woods with some friends of his, drank bottled martinis, and smoked Marlboro reds. I, of course, had thought myself eminently cool to be hanging out with college kids.

Zach's headlights appeared in the driveway, and he and Annie walked into the house together. Annie's hair was disheveled, and the mascara she'd applied so expertly earlier that evening now looked like small caterpillars nestled under each eye. Her pallor resembled Wicked-Witch-of-the-West green.

"How are you doing?" I asked her.

"Terrible. And I feel so stupid. I just want to go to bed."

"Okay, we'll talk about this tomorrow."

I thanked Zach as he left and then helped Annie navigate the hallway to her bedroom. I pulled back the bedcovers and tucked her in, clothes and all.

"Mom, the room's spinning."

"I know, sweetie."

• • •

Annie slept in later than usual the next day. Then she, her dad, and I had our talk at the kitchen table.

"So tell us about last night," I said.

"Uhhhh. I never, ever want to feel like this again. My head is killing me. I must say, though, I had a pretty good time before I got sick."

"That's why people drink," Pete said. "It's fun, and it loosens everybody up at a party. The trick is not to overdo it. You need to know when to stop."

"You'll see lots of drinking in college," I said, "and I'm guessing you'll partake in some of it. I'm not an idiot; I know college kids drink. I used to be one of them." I sipped my coffee as I pondered how best to make an impression on my daughter. "You'll soon be out of the house and away from our rules. It will be your rules then. You need to decide who and what you want to be."

"You guys don't have to worry about me. It's not like one night is going to turn me into an alcoholic or anything."

"Of course not. But alcoholism does run in families. You know my dad became an alcoholic in his later years, and your Nana Louise — well, you know how much she loves her Manhattans."

"Haha, yeah, I know."

"You'll see drugs in college too. Especially marijuana, so just be ..."

"I know, I know. You've been telling me this stuff for years. I *know.*"

It was hypocritical for me to tell Annie to stay away from pot. I hadn't. But knowing that kids tend to push back against their parents' rules, I always presented a conservative position. I wasn't trying to hide anything. I just felt that too much information about my own teenage drinking or pot use would have the net effect of giving her permission to do the same. And I didn't want that. There were times I had driven under the influence when I shouldn't have, and choices I'd made that I still regret.

I was first introduced to marijuana by my high school boy-friend, Craig, sitting atop a cliff of boulders one night high in the Santa Cruz Mountains. I didn't feel the least bit fazed by it and wondered what all the hoopla was about—until weeks later when he and I made a batch of "special" brownies. They were more weed than brownie, and the resulting feeling was an overwhelming sense of inertia. I didn't like it at all. It still seems paradoxical that being stoned is called a "high." It felt more like a "stupid."

I smoked a bit in college too, but not much. It was just part of the culture at the time, a coming-of-age thing, I guess. I was pretty square at heart when it came to drugs and never felt drawn to experiment further. My boyfriend, on the other hand, ultimately dove headfirst into the white stuff.

• • •

Annie's first drinking binge happened just before the end of her school days. I couldn't believe we were there already. It hadn't been easy—she'd always been such an enigma, so full of contradictions—but she certainly hadn't qualified as a problem child. In fact, her high school years were a wonderful time for me. In spite of occasional drama and bigger-than-life emotions, I had more fun with Annie than with almost anyone else. Strong willed and emotional, she was nevertheless a girl with an irresistible, playful innocence.

During that time, she coined a pet name for me. It began as "Woman," with no disrespect intended. She sang the word "Woooo-man," which ultimately morphed into "Woom." Funny thing is, she started to call Pete "Woman" too. She'd turn heads in public when calling out to her father, "Hey, Woman!" Over time, Pete and I collectively became "Wooms."

Back then, I believed I could keep Annie's issues with intermittent depression at bay through the very will of my mother love. By staying close, we two became enmeshed. Annie shared her life with me openly. While I wasn't foolish enough to think she told me everything, nor should she have, I'd enjoyed my role as confidante.

Whenever Annie and I went out together, whether for a meal, to the mall, or to the movies, she'd slip her arm through mine and we'd stroll side by side. "You're my hero," she sometimes said.

I could hardly believe my good fortune. Annie was mine. I thought myself to be the luckiest Woom in the world.

She would soon move away to begin college, and I prepared myself to let go. I'd always been the one to prop up my sensitive girl when life was hard—*would she now be able to do that for herself?* I began to pray for her and for her protection. I prayed that the faith I'd tried to instill in her throughout her life would see her through. I prayed to the God I'd come to know and love many years before.

• • •

When we first moved to Bend, I came with the agenda not only to change our family's lifestyle but also to explore my spirituality. I wasn't sure how this was going to manifest, but like most of us at one time or another, I was curious about God. Was he real, and what significance might he have for my life?

I'd participated in Young Life as a teenager, mostly for the cute boys, and I'd occasionally gone to church with my mom. She had an eclectic faith that attempted to reconcile her status as black sheep in her puritanical Pennsylvania Dutch family. She did, after all, consume alcohol and had become one of those nutty sun-worshiping Californians. Mom also sought understanding as to why she'd been ill most of her life. She'd been diagnosed with systemic lupus when I was five, and ministers visited our home as frequently as the doctor did.

It wasn't until I was in my late thirties and parenting a three-year-old and an eight-year-old that I began to seriously consider God. I tortured my officemate Jeanine for weeks with an endless barrage of questions about her Christian faith, and she finally threw up her hands in exasperation.

"Barbara, your questions! I will never be able to answer all of them to your satisfaction. Go ask him yourself!"

And that's exactly what I did. I went to the Horse himself. I began to pray.

"Hello, God ... Jesus? Are you real? If you are real, please reveal yourself to me."

Praying wasn't something I was comfortable with. Just hearing the words *Jesus* or *Bible* tended to startle me. When I first ventured into our local Christian bookstore, I felt miserably exposed and was sure the store clerks could read "Beware: Sinner" stamped on my forehead. When one young girl offered assistance, I flinched.

"Can I help you find something?" she asked.

"Well ... I think I'd like to buy a Bible," I said. The word *Bible* nearly stuck on my tongue. "Something for beginners, maybe?"

My helper shouted across the room to a clerk on the other side of the store who was stocking shelves. "Melissa, do you know where they moved the study Bibles?"

My face reddened. "If you don't know where they are, that's okay," I said. "I can come back later. It's no big deal."

"Oh, it's no problem," she bellowed. "We'll find you a Bible!"

What was it about that word that made me so uncomfortable? It's not like we were in Walmart and she was on the public address system directing me to the personal products kiosk. I'd just never been around people who said *Bible* quite so confidently—or so loudly.

Back at home, I continued to pray. "Jesus, if you're real, I want to know you."

There'd been a time when I believed all Christians were unsophisticated and simpleminded people. Yet I began to encounter credible people with a no-nonsense faith. It seemed that whomever I met in our new town, from our day care provider to the carpet cleaner to the lady in the craft store, everyone was talking about Jesus. And they were all pointing to one church in particular.

I began to think I'd moved to a town that was at the center of a major Christian revival, when actually nothing could have been further from the truth. Oregon is, in fact, one of the least-churched states in the country, and our county one of the least-churched counties in the state.

The more I prayed, the more comfortable I became with Jesus' name and the word *Bible*. One Sunday morning I felt bold enough to check out the church I'd been hearing so much about.

"I'm going to church!" I announced to my family, the three of them parked in front of the TV watching cartoons and eating Eggos. Pete only briefly acknowledged my exit.

"Okay, hon. Have fun," he said. At least he didn't roll his eyes.

I was on a mission that morning, in spite of the fact that I drove over Jeff's red tricycle backing out of the garage. It was May, with morning frost still on the ground, and jumping out of the driver's seat to deal with the obstruction annoyed me. I stooped to grab the trike and heaved it into the juniper bushes, muttering a multitude of unholy things. The tricycle survived, but I wasn't sure if I would.

I hoped it wouldn't always be this hard to get to church.

My efforts were rewarded, though. I'd never been to a church quite like this. It quickly became my new favorite place. The pastor was dapper and good-looking in a sharp shirt and tie. He was smart and funny too, not at all like the grim old guys in long robes I'd always associated with the pulpit. We sat in comfortable chairs, not pews. And the congregation was relaxed, free to laugh and cry and clap, and even turn around. Growing up, my mom had told me to always face forward, because it was impolite to turn around in church and look at the people behind you. Not so in this place. And there were hands high in the air during worship.

For someone still too uptight to say *Bible*, raising hands was a bit out of my comfort zone, but I loved to watch.

Oh, and God—he was there too. The presence of something, or Someone, great was unmistakable.

Over time, I came to know God in a way I hadn't thought possible. I'd found him, or he had found me, and I came to see how he'd been courting me for years. I was in love, and I began to experience small gifts from God as he wooed me. I finally bought a Bible, and even read it. Well, mostly. I put Annie and Jeff in Sunday school and was able to drag Pete along to church every now and then. Even my husband, whom I jokingly call "the Heathen," agreed there was something special going on in that place.

My decision to love God didn't happen all at once. There wasn't one event or one "born again" moment. Being the logical, left-brained person that I am, there were many questions to be answered. Questions like, did a big fish actually swallow Jonah and then spit him out days later, still fully alive? *Really?* And what about the apostle Paul, who instructed wives to submit to their husbands? That one could be a deal breaker for me. There was also the important matter that my brother is gay. How was I to reconcile the conventional Christian position on homosexuality with one of the finest people I know? I ultimately decided to leave my questions in abeyance, at least for a time, and just go for Jesus. I didn't jump into the pool all at once, but inched into the water one toe at a time, and then one limb at a time.

My love affair with Jesus deepened. Not counting my children's fledgling faith, I was the only Bible-thumping Christian in my entire extended family and among most of my longtime friends. I was the one tapped to say grace at the holiday dinner table, answer the biblical questions on *Jeopardy,* or pray for a friend of a friend who was sick. I was the one with "connections."

A couple of years later, I asked to be baptized, much to my mother's chagrin since I'd already been baptized as an infant. But I wanted baptism in the presence of faith. Annie asked to be baptized along with me. I thought she was too young at ten, but I wasn't going to impede any honest faith walk she wanted to take. So we went into the dunking pool together, with five-year-old Jeff looking on, sprawled on the steps leading up to the altar.

"Wow, that was weird," Annie said as she came up out of the water. "It feels like you're dying." She got it without me even having to tell her.

I've never been one to evangelize much, but I do share my faith when I feel a tug to do so. In those early days I'd always get stuck on the inevitable sixty-four-dollar question: "If God's so great, why is there so much suffering in the world?" I felt most of the canned, Christianese responses just didn't cut it. "It's God's will"; "it's a fallen world"; etc. — not very satisfying answers. Anyway, how should I know? What did I know of true suffering?

I secretly wondered if my God would hold up if I ever truly needed him.

# CHAPTER 3

⇀•↽

# Burgundy and Gold

The morning Annie left for college, Pete paced the length of our driveway, glaring at his watch. He and Annie were about to head south through the barren landscape of western Nevada and down into Arizona. They would caravan with Jasmine and her family, the friend Annie would room with at Arizona State. Because there was no space for Jeff and me in our bulging Expedition SUV, the two of us would fly down and rendezvous with the group in three days.

Pete was anxious to get on the road, so with no sign of Annie, I finally drove to Zach's to fetch her. There I found the two of them entwined, a snotty, sobbing mess. I had to pry Annie away and stuff her into the car.

In my mind, leaving for her freshman year of college should have produced a buzz of excitement, but Annie was a train wreck. During the short drive back to our house, I found myself trying to convince her all over again that her college years would be her best, and while she might feel apprehensive now, her anxiety and sadness would soon give way to the experiences of a lifetime.

I surveyed her distress and the significance of the grand passage taking place that day. It was impossible not to rewind my memory's videotape and reflect on my own departure for college thirty

*-41-*

years before. I was just shy of eighteen when my dad handed over the keys of our family car to my boyfriend of nearly two years. My parents trusted Craig and me to make that five-hundred-mile trip alone.

Now a mother myself, I winced at the memory. How could my parents have let me go like that? How could they send me out into the world without safely delivering me themselves? Why hadn't Mom needed to unwrap the new bed linens for my dorm room and prepare the place where I'd sleep each night? Why hadn't both Mom and Dad needed to hold me that one last time on the steps of the dorm, choking back those embarrassing tears of pride, grief, and celebration?

I needed to do all of those things. I needed to be on the launchpad right beside Annie, fluffing her pillow for a safe landing and positioning Band-Aids, ibuprofen, and a fire extinguisher within easy reach. I couldn't—wouldn't—miss it.

Arizona State had been on Annie's short list of potential colleges. When her good friend Jasmine decided to enroll there, the idea of leaving home with someone she knew helped quell her fears. Annie was suddenly excited about the prospect of college, and so were Pete and I. We felt this was an important next step for her, and we really didn't care where she went to school—just that she did.

Within minutes of Pete's arrival in Phoenix, the starched burgundy-and-gold cap he bought was his new favorite. He sports a baseball cap whenever he leaves the house, and I imagined he'd hear shouts of "Go Sun Devils!" even up in Oregon. I was sure the hat would soon be tattered from constant wear.

Any parent who has driven away from campus after depositing their college freshman into the dorm knows that feeling of loss and uncertainty. Is she ready? Will she be okay? What have we forgotten? Will she miss us? When I kissed Annie good-bye that day, I sent up silent prayers as I pressed my burning face next to hers, fighting back hot tears.

"Be good. Have fun. Call me."

• • •

Back home in Bend, Pete, Jeff, and I settled into our new routine. This was Jeff's first time in the role of "only child," and I looked forward to exclusive time with him, uninterrupted by Annie's drama and her bigger-than-life presence. But I missed her desperately. Sometimes I slipped into her bedroom and sat on the foot of her bed, trying to capture some remnant of her.

Annie had been gone for only a couple of weeks when Jasmine's mother called me.

"Barb, this is kind of a tough call to make," Sandra said, "but there's something you need to know. Jasmine told me that Anna's been mixing alcohol and Vicodin. I guess it made her pretty sick the other night. She was throwing up."

"What? Are you sure about this? Her doctor gave her a Vicodin prescription for cramps right before the girls left for school, but are you saying Annie's using it recreationally?"

"Well, Jasmine sure seems to think so, and she was worried enough to mention it to me."

This just didn't ring true. Annie could sometimes be unthinking and careless, but drugs were not her thing. And if it *was* true that Annie was experimenting, what was I going to do about it?

The next time Annie and I talked, I was relieved when she offered an unsolicited account of the story.

"So, Mom, I took some of that Vicodin my doctor gave me—which didn't work very well, by the way; my cramps are kicking my butt—but anyway, I forgot about it and then had a couple beers. Talk about la-la land."

"Annie, I don't even know what to say. Those two things combined can be deadly."

"I know, I know. I'm a complete moron. But don't worry—I won't be doing that again."

"*Be careful.* I don't know what your doctor was thinking giving a college freshman a prescription like that."

"Yeah, really. There are kids around here who pay for that stuff."

"Annie ... you wouldn't ..."

"Of course not! Mom, you know me better than that."

"Good. Just take good care of yourself. So how are your classes going?"

"Fine. I've got it covered. Don't worry. I promise I'll make you proud."

"This is your life. Forget about making me proud. Make yourself proud."

Over the next several weeks, it became apparent that Annie didn't have *any* of it covered. Jasmine was now spending all of her time with a new boyfriend. To quell her loneliness and fill the familiar void, Annie also turned to boys, her trusty pastime, and to her new best friend, alcohol. Boys were everywhere, living next door and across the hall, and alcohol was practically coming out the faucets at this party school.

For a girl who'd had her first drink just months before, Annie sure seemed to have become an adept drinker. I could hear it in her voice and see it in her emails: stories of frat parties, Mardi Gras, and dorm-room blowouts. I also experienced it in my inability to reach her by phone, day or night. It seemed she napped all day and carried on all night. Email became the only means by which Annie and I communicated.

> hi mom—i am feeling a little better today. classes are a must for tomorrow! the package arrived that you sent and i love it. so so cool. everyone has been coming to me saying, Trick or Treat and stealing my candy. you are too much. thankz a bunch mommy:) i think it's gonna be another late night tonight. Annie

> Annie—So glad you liked the goodies I sent. I'm concerned that you're burning the candle at both ends and not getting enough sleep. Please take care of yourself—and go to class! Love, Mom

I thought our email notes would become letters she'd cherish —treasured memories of those carefree days of young adulthood before the big responsibilities of life set in. Strangely, they are now the record of my daughter's teetering emotional balance and of a determined mother too far away to prevent the fall.

hey mom ... i feel like complete poop today. jasmine and her boyfriend are now officially "together" and now zach and i are off. i can't stand being here. everything makes me depressed. i'm tired of it all. i don't sleep, i hardly eat, and i can hardly hear myself think half the time ... well, i just needed to vent a little. that's all for now. luv you, bye, annie.

Hi Annie — You sound pretty low and that concerns me. I don't want to sound like I'm lecturing, but I'm wondering if you've stopped taking your meds. Can we please talk? Call me. I love you, Mom.

When I finally heard from her, Annie confided that she was now flunking the night class she'd been skipping. She also told me she thought alcohol was becoming a problem for her.

"You need to listen to your body," I told her. "You know how to have fun better than anyone I know. You don't need alcohol. Can't you just sip on a soda when you go out with friends?"

On top of all this, Annie became sick with a fever and nagging fatigue, and there was the ongoing problem of debilitating menstrual cramps, which even Vicodin didn't touch. Annie tried to finish papers and cram for tests, but she was unable to concentrate. She aced a Western Civ midterm but tanked on a chemistry exam.

It was an afternoon in late October when I received Annie's final email from ASU:

i am going crazy. i can hardly see the words i am typing i am crying so hard. why am i not good enough mommy? what am i supposed to do now? i feel lost and alone and sad and like total [crap]. help me please ... i feel nauseous, i can't sit still, and can't stop crying. i need to do something but i can't. annie. p.s. what can i do?

I was on the phone in an instant.

"Annie, I just saw your email. You don't sound so good. What's going on?"

"I'm just sittin' here on the floor of my room. Why is everything so screwed up?"

"I don't know, sweetie, but we'll sort it out. You'll feel better soon. I promise. Why don't you call Jasmine and see if she can come back to the dorm?"

"She won't come."

"Of course she will. Jasmine cares about you. I'll stay by the phone, and you let me know when she gets there. Okay?"

By the time we finished talking, my pulse was racing like a runaway train. I moved across the room and dropped onto the couch next to Pete.

"Annie, Annie, Annie," he lamented, as if she was hovering in the space above us. "What are we going to do with you?"

"I don't know how to help her." I leaned into his body. "I just assumed she'd adjust to college the way you and I both did. Everybody hits a few speed bumps that first year, but what is it about Annie that makes her come so unglued?"

The phone rang about an hour later. It was Jasmine. "Annie called me, and I'm here with her now. She isn't doing so great. She can't stop crying, and she's making cuts on her wrists with a pair of scissors. This is kind of freaking me out—what do you want me to do?"

*Oh, God, not that.* I knew a little about cutting because Annie had had a friend who'd done some self-injury—cutting and burning. All I could remember was that it had something to do with seeking relief from emotional pain by creating a physical outlet.

"Jasmine, I don't know exactly what's going on, but Annie needs help. Do you have access to a car, and can you get her to an ER? I just want to be sure she's safe."

I was the voice of reason and control, but inside I was quivering. We'd just crossed a threshold into new territory with Annie.

I spent the next hours on the phone with the ER doctor, and then with Jasmine again, and Annie too. She was exhausted by this time and had calmed down considerably. The doctor wanted to send her back to the dorm, which I thought was a terrible idea. Annie said she wasn't ready for that either. She wanted to stay in the hospital, and I wanted her there too, at least until I could get to Phoenix. The hospital couldn't admit her into one of the regular wards, however, so she was transferred to the nearby psych unit. Now technically an adult, Annie admitted herself.

I was up all night—obsessing, pacing, catastrophizing. I'd also been on the phone with Jasmine's parents. Pete got me to the airport at 4:00 a.m. for the first flight out, and then he returned home to stay with Jeff and to watch over our business.

• • •

I arrived in a cab at the front entrance of the psychiatric hospital in Phoenix at about ten o'clock that morning. When I asked at the front desk to see my daughter, I was told I had to wait for authorization. Apparently being Annie's mother was not authority enough, so I unleashed a diatribe about traveling all night to come rescue my daughter. The poor counter clerk nearly had to duck as I spewed. This was my first experience navigating HIPAA rules and the resulting insanity of trying to advocate for an adult child with a health problem. Except in the eyes of the law, Annie was anything but an adult.

I didn't know what I'd find when I finally did get to see my daughter, but my heart turned to mush at the sight of her. She was still asleep when I entered the dismal, darkened, yellow room that would have depressed even the smiley-face icon. I sat gently on the edge of the bed and nudged her.

"Hi, sweetie."

"Hi, Mom," Annie said as she forced her eyes open and yawned. "You came."

"Of course I came. How are you?"

"Okay, I guess. I'm pretty embarrassed about all of this."

It was then that I noticed the tender white skin on the underside of her forearms. It wasn't as bad as I expected. There were no bandages, and the cuts were superficial, but there were a lot of them—on both arms. She'd made these perfect little marks, exactly perpendicular to her extended arm—about five or six of them on each arm, at quarter-inch intervals. Each was about an inch and a half long.

"What's this about?" I gently lifted her arm.

"I dunno. It kinda made me feel better. It was just something to do."

"Annie, let's get you home. You need help with this, and it's obvious you're depressed again. We need to get your meds titrated, and when you're strong again, you can try college closer to home. Sound okay to you?"

"I'm sorry to be such a pain, Mom. Why am I such a mess?"

"I don't know, sweetie, but you're *my* mess, and I love you. Just because you're eighteen doesn't mean you were ready for all of this."

While Annie dressed, and her shoelaces and belt were returned to her, I spoke briefly with the woman psychiatrist who'd handled her case that night.

"Your daughter has poor coping skills," was the highly technical diagnosis offered, "but I think she can go back to school now." The doctor then signed off on Annie's discharge papers, and as she took my hand to say good-bye, she offered one final insight.

"Kids ..." She shook her head as if we were both members of the same clueless club.

Back to school? I didn't think so. We couldn't do that to Jasmine, and I couldn't do that to myself. I needed to keep an eye on my girl.

# CHAPTER 4

# Yellow and Green

Annie was treated for depression once she was back home in Bend. She returned to school in winter term, this time at our local community college. There she excelled in preveterinary studies, taking a full series of calculus, physics, and other sciences. She worked part-time in retail, and after six months of living at home, she moved across town into a rental house with another girl. A gorgeous new boyfriend entered the picture.

The traumatic events at Arizona State were now a distant memory. I knew that if we could just get Annie centered again and provide a family safety net for her to grow up some more, she'd finally be on her way. While Annie's emotions were still somewhat labile, she was fully functional and demonstrated a solid work ethic, both at school and on the job.

When the relationship with that boyfriend finally ran its course, Annie took stock. At age twenty she decided it was time to venture out again. Pete and I agreed she was ready.

She applied to the University of Oregon in Eugene with the intention of studying both music and science. Her anticipated start in the fall would be two years since that first semester away in Arizona, and this time her colors would be yellow and green. A UO grad himself, Pete already had the hat.

Once again, however, there was an ominous sign that all was not as well as it seemed. Annie was fired that summer from a second part-time job she'd secured at a local golf course. She'd been drinking on the job while she shuttled rowdy tournament players in golf carts between the greens and the watering hole at the clubhouse. It broke all the rules of common sense.

Our high hopes for Annie officially crashed after she moved to Eugene. The University of Oregon was a virtual rerun of Arizona State—too much partying and too many boys. Her emotions ran amok. She exhibited increasingly chaotic and sometimes risky behavior. She completed the fall quarter, barely, but with assurances from her to "do better next time," Pete and I reluctantly forked over tuition for the following quarter.

Annie was out every night while home during that Christmas break, sometimes returning in the wee hours of the morning in the car of a designated driver, and even a couple of times in the back of a cab. My concerns about her obvious excesses with alcohol escalated. Funny thing is, we never saw Annie drink. Now that she was just months shy of twenty-one, Pete and I occasionally offered her a beer or a glass of wine. It was always refused.

I did try to talk with her about all the partying.

"Annie, I know you're an adult now, but I'm really concerned about all this drinking."

"Oh, Mom, you worry too much. You know I've always been a late bloomer. I'm probably just making up for lost time. I know I need to take a break, but we have to talk about this later. I gotta go. I won't be out late, I promise. And I'm not planning to drink tonight. Love you!" With that I received a peck on the cheek and she was out the door.

It was 2:00 a.m. when she returned. Hearing the click of the latch on the front door, I dragged myself out of bed and met her in the doorway of her room.

"Annie, are you okay?" I asked.

"Yeah, I guess so." She staggered as she stepped into her pajama bottoms. Her eyes were glazed in a way I'd never seen before.

"You didn't drive home, did you?"

"No, I got a ride. But I really screwed up tonight."

"What do you mean? What happened?"

"Oh, never mind. It's nothing. I just have a bunch of people mad at me is all. Too much Jack and Coke, I guess."

"I thought you weren't going to drink tonight."

"Yeah, well ..."

"Think the damage can be repaired?" I asked.

"I dunno. I don't want to talk about it. I just want to go to bed."

"You've been saying, 'I don't want to talk about it' for as long as I can remember. There's going to come a time when you'll *have* to talk about it, Annie. These issues aren't just going to disappear."

"I know, I know. Good night, Mom. Love you."

• • •

That fall I followed a good friend to a new church that was forming in Bend. Suddenly weary of the invisibility I felt at the big congregation I'd loved for so many years, I now sat among friends and enjoyed the intimacy of a small church family. What impressed me most was how real everyone was, and I loved coming forward to receive Communion by intinction. We tore bread from the same loaf and dipped that sacred symbol of Christ's body into the same cup. It was so personal. I bawled every time.

There were also not one but two young single women in regular attendance at the new church who were pregnant at the time. While some congregations would have cast disparagement, these women were welcomed and embraced without judgment. I didn't realize at the time how important to me that attitude would later become.

• • •

Annie returned to school in Eugene for winter quarter. During those next months, the phone rang at all hours of the night. I'd startle awake from a deep sleep, and my heart would race with the sudden shock to my system. I'd anxiously attempt to coax Annie out of the eye of whatever storm she was in, then lie in a torrent of worry until morning.

There were also times I awakened to the shrill ring of a telephone, only to discover no one on the line. Had I dreamt the sound? With no memory of a dream—just nothingness jolted into wakefulness—I began to wonder if God might be waking me to prompt prayer. I had friends who'd experienced this, and it made me wonder.

After another of these episodes, I later called Annie to see what, if anything, she'd been doing at three that morning.

"It's weird you should ask," she said. "I was walking back to my apartment then. I was wet and miserable and cried the whole way."

"What were you doing out alone at 3:00 a.m.—are you trying to get yourself killed?"

"My ride left the party without me, so I had to walk home."

Another call, a real one, came in March.

"Hi, this is Megan." The clock by my bedside read 2:00 a.m. "I'm Anna's friend at school. She's really freaking out and wants you here." I could hear Annie's voice in the background, and she sounded combative.

"Anna's threatening to hurt herself with a knife, and we can't make her stop. She wants you to come."

Since we'd been through the cutting drill before, I didn't have fears of suicide, but I knew we needed to figure out once and for all what was wrong with Annie. I rallied Pete out of bed, and we were out the door.

Driving the mountain passes of Oregon can be dangerous under the best of conditions, and especially so in the dark and on icy pavement. But with a full moon to guide us, Pete and I made it safely to Eugene in two and a half hours. The sun was coming up as we entered Annie's apartment and found her and her two friends sound asleep on the couch. They were draped across each other like exhausted puppies.

Annie returned with us to Bend, where her physician suggested a diagnosis of bipolar II disorder. I was perplexed. Annie was a depressive with bouts of agitation and knee-jerk behavior, but I'd never seen any mania. The doctor explained that bipolar II is characterized by hypomania—that is, mania that's below the surface. The National Institute of Mental Health defines bipolar II as "a pattern of depressive episodes, shifting back and forth with hypomanic episodes." Hypomania manifests mostly as sleeplessness, irritability, agitation, or anxiety.

When a consulting psychiatrist agreed with the diagnosis a week later, Annie reluctantly began a course of bipolar medication. She also insisted on returning to Eugene. Her time at home had caused two weeks of missed classes and then midterm exams, so her college quarter was now in shambles. She felt it impossible to catch up and was able to withdraw from all of her classes without academic consequences. It was, however, too late for a tuition refund, and she'd missed the deadline to register for spring quarter.

Still referring to his favored Arizona State Sun Devil's baseball cap as his "fifteen-thousand-dollar hat," Pete now lamented that we were underwater with the Oregon Ducks.

There were still several months left on Annie's apartment lease in Eugene, which Pete and I had prepaid in full at the beginning of the school year. We agreed Annie could remain living there as long as she secured a job to earn the rest of her living expenses. Our agreement also stipulated that she attend regular sessions with a therapist and receive medical supervision for the new medications she was taking.

Over those next weeks and months, Annie's contact with us lessened. The daughter who had once been playful and open had now become secretive and contentious. She no longer seemed to want or need us. While family had once been everything to her, new friends now occupied that privileged space in her life. Many of those friends weren't even college students, and I couldn't wrap my mind around it.

I began to feel I was losing Annie and hated what this bipolar thing was doing to her. Was she taking her meds, and if so, were they even the right ones? Was she getting to her therapy appointments? Because she was no longer a minor, it was difficult for us to track this. We didn't know how hard she was looking for a job, or if she was even capable of the task. Was there more we could be doing—should be doing—to help her? Were we helping *too* much?

• • •

In early May I decided to make a surprise appearance in Eugene and see for myself what was going on. Under the pretense of a business trip to see one of my clients, I gave Annie only half a day's notice of my arrival and then checked into a hotel.

When I visited her later in the day, what I found shocked me. The cute apartment, with the sunny picture window and bright decor, we'd decorated together just eight months before now sat cloaked in darkness behind drawn draperies. It looked like the postapocalyptic scene of a party gone terribly wrong. Remnants of fast food were everywhere, and every glass and dish from the cupboards lay dirty and stacked in piles throughout the kitchen and living room. Overstuffed bags of garbage and empty beer cans were strewn on the kitchen floor, and as I peered into the adjacent bedroom, I could see Annie's clothes littering every square inch of floor space. I didn't have to eyeball the cat box in the far corner to know it was there.

"Annie, how can you live like this?"

"I'm a college student. Give me a break."

"You mean you *used* to be a college student."

"*Anyway*, my friend Porter is practically living on the couch now, so a lot of this mess is his."

I eyed an ashtray on the end table near where I was standing and picked it up for a closer look. Annie didn't smoke, at least not that I knew of. In the ashtray were a few small "roaches," remnants of marijuana cigarettes.

"Do these belong to Porter?"

"Mostly," she replied. "I smoke a little. Sometimes."

"When did you start this? I thought you hated this kind of thing, and what about your voice?"

"You know, it's really not your business. And you're the one who just showed up here. I would have cleaned up if I'd had more notice."

Annie's comment was like an arrow through the heart. *Her life not my business?* "Well, you're living a life that we still pay for, and up until a couple of months ago, you were a full-time student on our nickel. I think that makes some of your choices our business."

"It's always about the money with you, isn't it, Mom?"

"Where did that come from? It's *never* about the money. But when you're still financially dependent, I think we get a vote. And maybe some respect." I couldn't believe Annie was talking to me like that. I could feel my emotional temperature rising. I wasn't sure which was worse—Annie's disrespect or the chasm I felt building between us.

We continued to argue. I felt she needed to get a job. She was an adult, and if she wasn't in school, she needed to pay her own way. Annie countered that there were no jobs in Eugene. The conversation exhausted me.

She then switched gears. "So, Mom, about my car ..."

"Uh, what about your car?"

"It's in the shop. Porter drove it one night, and it got sort of dinged. But don't worry, we didn't even report it to the insurance company. Porter's paying cash for the whole thing."

"Well, this just gets better and better. Just how *dinged* is your car?"

"Porter hit a parked car, and in case you're wondering, yes, he'd been drinking. That's why we didn't report it. It pretty much munched the front right fender, and repairs are gonna cost about fifteen hundred dollars."

"He was drinking, and you let him drive your car?"

"He borrows my car a lot. I didn't even know he'd been drinking."

"Annie, Annie. This isn't good." I summoned all the composure I could muster. "First, you shouldn't be loaning out your car, and secondly, how is an unemployed college student going to pay for this?"

"His parents are sending him the money. An uncle or something owns a body shop, and we got a really good deal. The repairs are nearly done, and I can have my car back when the money gets here."

At this point, I was sitting at the kitchen table with my hands holding my face together. "Your dad's gonna go absolutely ape when he hears this. Do you really think that this guy's parents are going to send him that kind of money to repair someone else's car?"

"You don't have to worry about Porter. He's taking this very seriously, and he doesn't want any trouble that could affect his future. He's going to be a doctor, Mom."

"Well, that makes me feel better," I said. "They let drunks be doctors now?"

"That's not fair! You should be happy I've just taken care of this and didn't have to involve you guys. I thought you'd be proud of me."

Somehow I seriously doubted Annie's motive was to help her dad and me. I was feeling manipulated, and it made me angry. "Our name's on that car, and we should have been involved in the repairs."

"We'll take care of it. You'll see."

Annie and I had dinner together, and I went back to my hotel room alone. She showed up at ten the next morning, having been up all night. *Mania?*

I returned home later that day feeling as worried as when I arrived. Annie just wasn't the same. Was all of it just the chaotic antics of an enigmatic twenty-year-old trying to figure out life, or was mental illness claiming my daughter? Maybe it was just delayed teenage rebellion. Whatever the case, she didn't have a job, and Pete and I wondered if it was time to pull the plug on the apartment or the car, and force Annie to come back to Bend. Would she even come back?

What were we supposed to do?

➤•⤝

# CHAPTER 5

# Center of
# the Universe

Much to my surprise, Porter did come through with the money for the car repairs a couple of weeks later. The Camry was released to Annie, good as new. She also reported she was now sporting the uniform of a fast-food restaurant chain, a fact that gave me a twinge of regret. I had always thought she was too good for a job like that, but if it was going to pay her bills, maybe that was a lesson she needed to learn. It was probably a lesson I needed to learn as well.

Annie celebrated her twenty-first birthday in Eugene, the first big milestone in her life not shared with family. By this time there was a new boyfriend. James was a friend of Porter's, and he had just accepted an offer to attend an automotive trade school in Phoenix. Annie called us with the announcement that she planned to move there with him in late August.

"You're going back to Phoenix!" I didn't know whether to scream or cry. "Are you kidding? Have you even known this guy long enough to be making such an important decision?"

"James and I have been together for two months, Mom, and this is what I've decided to do."

"What about your health? I'd like to see you stay closer to home where we can help you. And what about school?"

"I've really lost interest in school for now, and I'll probably just get a job at a golf course or something. I'll take my meds with me. It'll be fine."

I thought the move was a terrible idea. Annie seemed so unstable. I was tempted to issue an ultimatum: *If you run off with this guy, it will ruin your life forever, and I'll never speak to you again!* Or maybe even bribery. But what could I possibly offer that would keep her in Oregon?

At a loss over how to deal with this, I scheduled a visit with Karen, the therapist who had done family counseling with us over the years. She'd also done some work with Annie in middle school, and then again after her meltdown at Arizona State. Karen cautioned me.

"We don't get a vote about who our adult children choose, Barb. If you contest Annie's choices, it could drive a wedge in your relationship forever. Parents are rarely the winners in these things. And even though her choices are not always well conceived and her transition to adulthood seems to be a rocky one, they are still her choices to make. You need to treat her like an adult, even if she may not be acting like one."

When Annie was young, my responsibilities seemed so clearcut. Now it was hard knowing when to intercede and when to let go. While an intelligent and competent human being, Annie had emotional issues that handicapped her in perplexing ways. I often tried to figure things out for her. When I saw her as unable to do something for herself, I often did it for her. And thought I did so brilliantly.

"I know your intentions are good," Karen said, "but you're not her therapist. It's not your job to take on some of the roles you have. You can't treat her depression or fix her life. She has to learn to deal with these issues on her own."

"But I love her so much. Isn't it my job to keep her safe?"

"Maybe Annie's been loved too much. I know it's scary to step back because of some of the things that have happened, but she must find her own way."

I didn't know how it would be possible to love someone too much. What did that mean, anyway? But Pete and I both saw the wisdom in Karen's advice. We heeded her warnings. Annie knew where we stood regarding the move to Phoenix with a guy she barely knew, but we didn't contest it further.

"It's your life," we told her.

Annie called us a couple of days before their scheduled departure. "Aren't you coming to Eugene to say good-bye to me?"

"I didn't know you wanted us to," I answered. I hated that Annie was moving out of state and we wouldn't have a chance to say good-bye, but it didn't seem like it should be up to us. "If you want to see the family before you leave, why don't you and James swing through Bend?"

"Bend is so out of our way, Mom. We're heading south on I-5 day after tomorrow."

"Well, sweetie, Eugene is so out of our way. Please drive safely and let us know when you get there." I hoped I wouldn't regret the telephone good-bye. "Oh, and Annie, remember that we love you, and we're always here for you."

"I know, Ma. I love you too."

Two days later, Annie and James rolled into our driveway. Seems she just couldn't leave without her family's send-off, and I was relieved. Maybe we weren't losing her after all.

• • •

James seemed wrong for Annie in so many ways, and I admit that some of my objections to him were superficial. The fact that he was significantly shorter than Annie's five-foot-eight-inch frame bugged me, and I didn't understand the attraction. There was also the matter that he was a graffiti artist, and while his work showed talent, to me it also showed disregard for the law. People who did that kind of thing just weren't part of my world.

It had never occurred to me before that my daughter might one day run off with a guy who didn't fit my vision for her. I wasn't exactly sure what that vision was, but I knew it wasn't this.

In spite of my reservations, I did find James quite likable. He seemed to genuinely care about Annie. I made him promise to call us if she ever had a problem, which he did three months later. He didn't want to, because Annie had already dumped him and was running amok with coworkers from the golf course where she worked. But she showed up back at his place one night, drunk and out of control. James asked for our help.

I called the Sun City police department from my cell phone, while he and I stayed connected on our landline. I soon heard sirens in the distance and then detected sounds of a skirmish when handcuffs were snapped onto Annie's wrists.

The police tried to deliver Annie to the emergency room of a nearby suburban hospital, but without her purse and proof of insurance, she was denied care. The two police officers then drove her an hour across town, where she was admitted to the county mental hospital.

Annie called her dad and me the next morning, absolutely grief stricken by what she'd experienced the night before.

"This is a terrible place. No one should ever have to stay in a place like this. Did you know that James called the cops on me?"

"I'm sorry you had to go through that, Annie. But it wasn't James who called the police. I did. He didn't know how to defuse the situation so he asked for our help. How are you feeling today?"

"Exhausted. Embarrassed."

It struck me as odd how "normal" Annie seemed that morning. I was beginning to think that maybe alcohol was playing a bigger role in her emotional life than a mood disorder. Whatever the case, I desperately wanted Annie home where I could take care of her, but with Karen's voice in my head, I willed myself to treat her like an adult.

"What are you going to do now?" I asked.

"There was only a twenty-four-hour hold on me, so I'll see if I still have a job and get on with things. You don't need to come get me."

"I wasn't planning on it," I said. "This is your life, and it's up to you to manage it."

• • •

Annie did call a week later, however, and asked to come home. Things were clearly over with James, and she admitted her drinking, and her life, was out of control. She wanted our help getting stabilized again and agreed to return to counseling. This time Pete flew the rescue mission, and he and Annie drove her car from Arizona back to Bend. It was nearly Christmas.

Annie hadn't lived at home for two years, and her return disrupted our otherwise calm existence. While I couldn't pinpoint the exact timing of the change, Annie was different. Her emotionality and vulnerability had turned into something else. She was more argumentative and caustic. The underlying sweetness in her seemed dormant.

There was discord especially over her comings and goings. At twenty-one, she certainly didn't need the answerability of curfew, but after years of turmoil, Pete and I were toughening in our resolve to not let her dominate our lives. We had the right to some peace and a good night's sleep, free from worry and late-night phone calls.

"If you're going to live here, Annie, you need to get a job and honor our rules," I told her. "I know you're used to being on your own, but I won't be able to sleep or function at work with you out until all hours of the night. I just need to know when to expect you, so let's make our agreements on a day-to-day basis. Okay?"

Annie complied until the night she called at 1:00 a.m. to tell me she'd be late. Like most mothers, I then lay awake until I saw her headlights in the driveway. A week later, when the first ice storm of the season hit and Annie missed the 2:00 a.m. accountability curfew we'd mutually decided on, I was done. She didn't call, didn't answer my calls, and when she walked through the front door the next day at noon with defiant arrogance, I exploded.

"Annie, you have exactly one week to find another place to live."

"I'm twenty-one. You can't expect me to keep a curfew!"

"I can have whatever rules I want in my own house, and I don't need to lose sleep because of your disregard for common courtesy." I slammed the newspaper I was holding onto the kitchen counter. "There was a winter storm warning out last night, and when you didn't come home as agreed, I was beside myself with worry. How dare you treat me with such disregard!"

"It's not my fault you can't sleep."

Her air of entitlement exasperated me. "You just don't get it, do you, Annie? This is not a hotel. You're an adult now and currently a guest in this house. If you want different rules, find a different place to live."

Shocked and furious, Annie packed a bag within minutes and headed for the door.

"You don't have to leave today," I said.

"Oh yes I do. I can't stand it here another minute."

"Well, okay then. May I please have your house key before you leave?"

"Uh, are you kidding me? You're really kicking me out?"

"As far as I'm concerned, you don't respect us enough to live here. And we really don't trust you right now."

We didn't see or hear from Annie for the next two weeks, and she rebuffed my attempts to reach her by phone. I was heartsick. When we ultimately reconnected in late January, she'd secured a job at an office supply store and was living on the couch at the home of an old friend from high school.

She still didn't see her own culpability in our asking her to leave. While she played victim to the hilt, I do think her wounding was real. Removing her from the center of the universe was painful for her, and for us, and at the time I wasn't altogether sure we'd even done the right thing. How does a parent ever know when making that kind of hard decision?

In a therapy session with Karen weeks later, she was incredulous when I relayed the details of the story. "I didn't know you had it in you, Barb," she said. "Good boundaries."

"I felt so manipulated. After all we've done for her—I was just so angry."

"Anger," she said, "sometimes helps."

# CHAPTER 6

# My Daughter the Drug Addict

By March we'd reconciled with Annie to the point that Pete and I agreed to fund the first month's rent for her new apartment. But soon afterward came that Easter Sunday when she confessed to me about her meth use. The surge of fear I'd felt that moment had become an all-consuming deluge in my soul.

I attempted regular check-ins with Annie. While she seemed peculiarly enamored with her new lifestyle, the fallout of her admitted drug use was already becoming apparent. Pete and I watched helplessly from afar as her life unraveled. Her rent for May was coming due, and without the roommate who had already bailed, prospects weren't good she'd be able to cover the amount on her own. There was also the matter of a beast of a man who'd begun stalking her, letting himself into her apartment and sitting in wait for her return. He was reportedly the one who first gave her meth, and his asserted claim on her was frightening.

What were we to do? When Annie had moved into the apartment, Pete and I had made clear what her responsibilities in the matter would be. Could we now intervene by rescuing her once again? She needed help for sure, but what kind of help?

Mothers are supposed to know how to do these things. I used

to boast that I could hear my children's eyes open when they awakened in their beds. If I could do that, surely I could manage this. I'd been fixing things for years. This was just another bump in the road of parenting—albeit a big bump. I'd handle it. I would start by going to Annie and telling her just how much she was hurting her family and herself. I'd convince her she needed to stop all of this. I would bring her home, dust her off, dry her out, and get her pointed in the right direction—again. I would save her as I always had. While Pete and I were resolved not to pay Annie's rent, we would otherwise help her in any way she'd allow.

"Annie, let us help you walk away from this stuff," I told her. "Come home and hang out here for a week or so, and we'll help you figure this out. You can start over."

"I know—this craziness has to stop," she said. "Is it really okay if I come home for a while? This guy completely creeps me out."

With that, Annie appeared on our doorstep, reporting that she'd broken all her meth pipes, had told the beast good-bye, and was putting all of this behind her. Maybe I'd overestimated the severity of her situation. Things looked like they were going to be okay now. I was relieved.

Annie set up camp on the family room couch, positioning herself horizontally on the spot that had always been hers. Hypnotized by one TV show after another scrolling before her, she dozed in and out of consciousness for two days. Even as she slept, her presence seemed to suck all the air out of the room, and I was unable to coax her into a bedroom.

When she finally became vertical again, I made my pitch. "Glad to see you're making a rally, sweetie." I said. "How are you feeling? You ready to talk about what's next?"

"What do you mean 'what's next'?"

"Well, I just mean we need to talk about a plan so you can get back on track. I'm sure you don't want to lose your apartment or your job."

Her mood shifted instantly. "Why can't you people just leave me alone? It's because of you everything is all screwed up. None of this would have happened if you hadn't kicked me out."

"Hey, wait a minute. Those were choices you made," I protested. "I love you, and I want to help you with this. Let's work things out so you can move forward."

"The last thing I want to do is talk to you right now. Just leave me alone." Annie threw the blanket off her lap and leaped to her feet. "I'm getting out of here."

She made a quick call on the house phone and was out the door. Feeling helpless and aghast, I now had the sickening realization that my daughter wasn't done with meth. I didn't know much, but I did know it was calling her name, and she'd picked a fight with me in order to answer that call. It was eminently clear we were now facing a problem even a mother couldn't fix.

A new word appeared on my lips: *addict*. Had my daughter become a *drug addict*? If so, how could this be? Annie had been a pretty good kid. She'd been a lot of work, and there'd certainly been some rough spots, but none of it seemed predictive of meth. There was so much goodness in her. I felt sure that with time and growth, her frailties would strengthen and she'd be on her way. She had so much promise—she was just bursting with gifts to pour out onto the world.

Pete and I had been good parents. Not perfect, but we're good people. Whatever parenting mistakes we'd inevitably made, we made up for through sheer effort and determination to always be there for our kids. We were there for every school event, parent-teacher conference, T-ball and Little League game, Sunday school class, choir concert, and basketball game. We'd kissed every owie, caught every falling tear, slayed dragons under the bed, and wrestled monsters in the closet. I sewed every Halloween costume, packed every lunch. We dined on world map place mats and made geography fun. We counted falling stars on hot summer nights and huddled during winter power outages, making hand puppets on the ceiling by candlelight. We played games, read books, baked cookies, and had whipped cream wars in the kitchen. Pete and I were as forgiving as we were strict, and we were *always* there. We talked to our kids about absolutely everything—including drugs.

We were the family this could never have happened to. Never in the wildest, scariest, darkest places that my parental fears could take me did I think that Annie would ever experiment with hard drugs, let alone that drug use would come to define her life. Drug addicts were the dregs of society, scum, bottom-feeders—and they *certainly* didn't live in our part of town. They were inherently bad, awful people who couldn't control their urges or their lives. Right? They got themselves into this mess and deserved whatever happened to them. Society would be better off, and the world a better place, if they all just set sail together on a floating glacier somewhere in deepest Antarctica.

But if this were true, how could my Annie be one of them? Never had there been a child more wanted or more loved. How could my most precious daughter, into whom I'd poured a life-time of mother's love, be this vile thing? Had I failed at my life's work?

Like all parents, Pete and I had hopes and dreams for our child, none of which included a stopover in addiction. Where did things go wrong? Were there signs we'd missed, and if so, what could we have done about them? What did we leave out, forget, do too much of, or do wrong? I thought if I was an attentive and passion-ate mom, and if I dotted all the i's and crossed all the t's, checked all the to-do boxes, and poured out my love, the results would be guaranteed. I thought we could *make* our children into who they became. Great kids come from great families, and screwed-up kids come from screwed-up families. Right?

• • •

I wasn't sure I had the answers to all my questions, but I knew I had to do something. I had to save Annie. So I began by chasing after her.

Annie's apartment was about five miles from our house. I

drove by often just to see what I could see. The presence of her little black Camry was always a clue to whether or not she was getting to work. I also checked out the cars parked near hers, looking for signs of familiarity or danger. I was searching for any indication of how she might be doing, and in my own way I was just trying to be close to her.

Never one to visit unannounced, I occasionally called Annie's cell to see if I could swing by for a minute. Most of the time she didn't answer her phone, however, so I ultimately cast niceties aside and began to just show up at her door. The times Annie did come to the door, she wasn't particularly happy to see me. *We used to be so close.* It seemed she was always sleeping, even in the middle of the day. Wasn't she going to work? I'd be shooed away with promises of a call later.

Once, however, Annie invited me in. We sat at her kitchen table and chatted for a while. Her place was trashed. Dozens of empty liquor bottles lined the kitchen counters and were stacked up against the living room wall. They looked like trophies in various shapes, sizes, and colors.

Annie seemed softer than the last time we talked, and it felt good to be with her. She wasn't feeling very well, though, and now a smoker, she asked if I would dash to the store for her and pick up a pack of cigarettes. I confess that I did, and I paid for them too, knowing there was a promise of more time with her when I returned.

Most of the time when I drove to Annie's apartment, however, my knocks went unanswered. On one such morning, I left a pile of papers stacked on her porch by the front door, information about meth I'd printed from the Internet. They were stories of destroyed lives, with gruesome photos to prove it. The before-and-after mug shots showed the progression of meth addiction. Once healthy-looking, attractive people, the faces were now thin, pale, and wasted. Red sores dotted some, and dark holes gaped where teeth had once been. Hair was thinning and unkempt. Eyes were dark, sunken, lifeless. "The Faces of Meth"—surely these would get Annie's attention.★

I sent up a silent prayer as I laid the papers by the doorjamb. *God, please protect Annie—her beautiful face, her glistening hair.* Thoughts of darkened gums and rotting teeth in her perfect mouth sent pangs through my body that threatened to destroy me.

On the drive home, I eyed a large billboard at a congested intersection and vowed that should meth ultimately consume my daughter, I'd someday plaster Annie's before-and-after "Faces of Meth" photos on that very site, high above the traffic for all to see. Maybe others could be saved and would steer clear of the drug that had taken my Annie.

On another one of my unannounced visits to her apartment, I heard voices inside as I approached the door. When I knocked, there was silence.

"Annie ... Annie, are you in there? It's Mom. Can we please talk for a few minutes? Come on, Annie. Let me in."

I heard the slightest, whispered "shh," and then a crisp *click* on the lock. I sensed a stirring inside of several people and became convinced a drug deal was in progress inside. With my adrenaline pumping, I hightailed it to my car and called 911.

"I have reason to believe there's a drug deal under way at my daughter's apartment. She's begun using methamphetamine and needs to be stopped. Her address is ..."

It seemed a crazy gesture, but it was *doing* something. I figured desperate times called for desperate measures.

Annie called me the next day, raging that I'd nearly gotten her arrested.

"That was the point," I told her, indignant. Desperate measures indeed.

My inability to access my daughter, touch her, feel hope for

---

★See Joseph Rose, "The Faces of Meth," *Oregonian*, December 28, 2004, www.oregonlive.com/pacific-northwest-news/index.ssf/2004/12/the_faces_of_meth.html; Multnomah County Sheriff's Department, "Faces of Meth," www.facesofmeth.us/ (accessed March 14, 2014).

her, was almost more than I could bear. Sometimes I drove by her apartment at night, parked across the street, and watched the small window over Annie's kitchen sink just to try to catch a glimpse of her. My mother's colored vases were no longer in view on the windowsill. I wondered why she'd removed them. Was she removing all traces of the family from her life?

I never did see Annie on any of my stakeouts. I later learned I'd been watching an empty apartment—she'd moved on. When I tried to track her down at work, I was told she'd been fired because of too many absences.

All of this happened within two months of that Easter Sunday. Where in the world was she now?

Annie was gone, and there was nothing I could do about it. I hated the helplessness and hated her for giving it to me. How could she do this to us? I sometimes buried myself in Pete's chest and cried loud, heaving sobs. "What's going to happen to her? What's to become of us?" I needed to *do* something. I needed to find Annie and stop her. I needed to save our family.

I picked up the phone and started dialing. I began by looking for a drug hotline or help center, but could find none in our community. If meth was such a problem in Oregon, why wasn't anybody doing something about it? What were people like us supposed to do? I felt like my house was on fire and I couldn't even find a water pistol to help douse the flames.

A friend suggested I call the head of Central Oregon Drug Enforcement, a police captain who was a friend of her family. He proved to be a nice enough fellow, and I asked him to please find my daughter and set her straight about drugs. I told him about the big beast who'd been stalking Annie.

"She's with him?" he said. "He's dangerous—*crazy*, in fact. Been in and out of prison for years. He came after me once with his fists. He's one of the worst we're dealing with. She must be into things pretty deep."

Waves of fear pulsed through me, and all I could mutter were tormented expletives.

Next I called the sheriff. Then I called the undersheriff. I called a police sergeant. I called friends. I called friends of friends. And I called absolutely every listing in the Yellow Pages under "Addiction Services." This included treatment centers, outpatient drug counselors, and therapists. I sobbed out the details of our circumstances to everyone with whom I spoke and asked what we should do.

"There must be a protocol for this kind of thing. Just tell me what to do and I'll do it." Absolutely no one could answer questions to my satisfaction.

Didn't anybody understand? Didn't anybody get this wasn't who we were?

Annie was special. She wasn't really one of them. She didn't belong here.

None of us belonged here.

# CHAPTER 7

# Methmobile

My mood changed often. Some days I was grieving and gloomy, and others I was simply galled. I came to prefer anger to despair, the former providing more impetus for me to *do* something. On the despairing days I cried easily, and while not clinically depressed, I'd have quiet, dark nights when it felt like my soul was drifting. My angry days, on the other hand, at least fueled my energy.

I was now in an angry phase, and it was all about the car. We'd bought Annie her beautiful Camry shortly before she'd transferred to the University of Oregon, and at no time did our plans for it include "methmobile."

The old blue truck that Annie had been driving since high school could not be counted on for the sometimes treacherous winter driving across the Cascade Mountains. She'd needed something safe and reliable to navigate the pass on her trips home to Bend from Eugene, and at the time, the Camry was one of the safest cars on the road.

Pete insisted on a new car, with the accompanying warranties and dependability, and I wanted all the safety features—surround air bags, an anti-skid system, a roll bar, flotation devices, and an ejection seat with a parachute. When filling out the form with our wish list, we inadvertently ended up with nearly every upgrade the model provides. It was a gorgeous car—so much more than we ever should have given a twenty-year-old, and doing so was certainly one of our dumbest parenting blunders ever.

When the chaos in Annie's life escalated toward the end of that year in Eugene, Pete and I had transferred the car's title from our names to hers. We wanted to distance ourselves from any liability for her mistakes, but we did stay on as lien holders. Annie would never be able to sell the car without our permission, and our insurance agent told us we'd be informed of anything that ever happened to the car (if not our daughter). Because of its significant value, we kept the car insured, but in Annie's name. These changes would later prove invaluable when Annie's drug problem really took hold.

• • •

The first test of this strategy came in July when we received a letter from a local towing company that the Camry had been impounded. We hadn't heard from Annie for weeks, but learned through an accompanying police report that a cohort of hers had been pulled over for speeding while driving her car, and he was cited for driving without a license. Annie wasn't even in the car, yet it was impounded nonetheless and a $400 payment was required to claim it. The car could go to auction if the fine wasn't paid within thirty days.

Not knowing Annie's whereabouts, or her financial ability to rescue the car, Pete and I intervened. We got the car out of impound and then stashed it on the ranch of some friends east of town. Annie had a second key and could otherwise have easily retrieved the car out of our driveway.

Our intent was to use the car as leverage to finesse agreement from Annie to enter some kind of rehab program. We'd return the car after treatment was completed. But Annie was livid, and the ensuing phone calls from her were rages of a proportion I'd never seen or heard. She was saying things to me I would have thought sheer genetics might disallow a child from saying to her parent. I was deeply wounded and chose for a while to either refuse her calls altogether, most of which appeared as "blocked" on caller ID, or to abruptly conclude the conversation when she became abusive.

Pete and I became conflicted as to whether the car belonged to Annie or to us. We had paid for it but had given it to her. It was in her name, but only for our purposes. For good or for bad, we ultimately decided the proper thing to do was return the car to Annie, and we did so once she reimbursed us for the $400 impound fee. We had no idea where the money came from.

It wasn't long until Annie's car was impounded a second time and under similar circumstances to the first. Once again a male cohort was behind the wheel and pulled over for speeding, but this time Annie and two others were also in the car. The foursome, abandoned on the side of the road after the car was towed, flagged down a passerby they knew. The driver, a female acquaintance, was on her way to the jail to visit her boyfriend. She gave the four of them a lift. They waited in the parking lot while she went inside.

Meanwhile, back at impound, the police discovered stolen electronics the guys had left in the trunk of Annie's car. In a scene right out of the Keystone Cops, the four bungling perpetrators were arrested just steps outside the jail door and escorted inside. When booked, drugs were found in Annie's pockets. This was her first arrest, and from the looks of things, she wasn't a very adept criminal.

"Mom, you've got to get me out of here," Annie demanded with her first phone call home.

"I don't have to do anything, Annie. Sounds to me like you're where you need to be."

"Mom, please. I'm your daughter. You don't want me in jail, do you?"

"Of course I don't want you in jail, but I didn't put you there.

Your dad and I will take care of getting the car, and when you can pay us back for the impound, we'll return it to you again."

"Are you going to hide it like you did last time? That's *my* car, you know."

"We're the lien holders on a car that we paid for, Annie. If it's so important to you, then maybe you should take better care of it."

Pete and I got the car out of impound, again, and brought it home. Even though Annie was in jail, we knew she wouldn't be for long. Jail overcrowding was well publicized, and nonviolent offenders were often "matrixed" out within days, if not hours. We knew the impound yard had what was now Annie's only set of car keys, so we figured our garage would be safe enough storage until she had the money to repay us. Then we would return the car to her—again.

After the Camry sat untouched in our garage for several days, I finally found the will to crawl inside and confront whatever I might find. I slipped into the passenger seat and immediately felt the small chamber closing in on me. I steadied myself with a calming breath and began opening compartments to see what remnants of my daughter's life were inside.

The car was filthy. It smelled. There was almost a film on the interior roof and walls, giving it a sooty feel. I cautiously opened the center console, afraid of what might jump out at me, and found a couple of butane lighters and a clear glass pipe. I lifted the pipe and gingerly examined it, as if it were a gun that might go off at any moment.

The pipe was dirty inside, with both black and white burn marks. I imagined what it might be like to hold it when hot to the touch. What was the insidious power this device and its accompaniments had over my daughter? Had there been any trace left of the crystals that once occupied the small baggies I also found there, would I have felt compelled to find out? Recognizing the absurdity of the thought, a small thread of panic jolted through me. Was meth going to ruin us all?

I dropped the pipe into the empty brown bag I'd brought to

the car with me. Then went the baggies, lighters, empty cigarette boxes, scraps of paper, fast-food containers, and beer and soda cans I found strewn about the car. The brown bag went into the trash.

I was done cleaning up Annie's messes and otherwise left the car as is. I knew it would soon be back in her possession. I just hoped it would keep her safe.

I went into the house and returned with a cruet of olive oil. I slipped into the car again, this time in the driver's seat, and after dropping a bead of oil on my forefinger, made the sign of the cross on the steering wheel. I knew nothing about such things and had never anointed anything in my life, but I was now doing so to my daughter's car. It wasn't special oil from a Jewish temple or anything purchased from a Christian bookstore. It was just my cooking oil. I trusted that the God I loved and counted on for all things would bless it and would protect Annie.

I made another sign of the cross on the center of the dashboard, then got out of the car and made a final cross on the center front of the hood. I'd now done all I could do.

CHAPTER 8

✥

# Calling the Cops

Pete and I worked especially hard that year at the health care recruiting firm we own. Focus on business was a welcome distraction from the sadness that pervaded our home, and in terms of revenue, it was ironically our best year since we'd purchased our little company fifteen years before.

At the time, we rented a small suite of offices in a hundred-year-old brick mall in downtown Bend. It was just the two of us in our business, and Pete's office was right next to mine. Living together for thirty years, and working together for twenty, was a lot of, well, togetherness—but it was a workable formula for the privilege of calling a place like Bend home.

After yet another marathon day at work, I walked in the front door at home, tossed my purse onto the kitchen counter, and kicked off my shoes. Pete was close behind in his car, and he pulled into the driveway shortly after I did. *Ugh*, the dead bolt on the front door had been left unlocked again. Jeefffff . . .

It was August, and with a part-time job in retail, seventeen-year-old Jeff started work later than we did. He often charged out the door absentmindedly, neglecting to lock it behind him. He'd also leave the house lit up like a Christmas tree, not only with lights, but also with two TVs chattering at each other from opposite ends of the house. Annie wasn't the only one in the family with attention issues.

I climbed the stairs to our master bedroom to change clothes and found the door closed. *That's weird.* As I entered the room, the crime scene unfolded in front of me. One of the two sliding windows across the room was wide-open, as were the doors to my armoire, where I kept all of my jewelry. I stood there for a moment, stunned, trying to interpret what I was seeing. Finally it registered: *Annie.*

I dashed across the room to the clothes hamper where just two weeks before I'd stashed the carved wooden box that contained all of my treasured jewelry. Having just learned that addicts often steal from their families, I'd wanted to be prepared and had buried my jewelry under our dirty laundry. I hadn't believed for a minute that Annie would really steal from us, but should the unthinkable happen, Annie wouldn't look there. I was relieved now to discover she hadn't.

My emerald engagement ring was in that box, as was an anniversary ring my dad had given Mom. My grandmother's tiny wedding set that would have fit a child's finger was in there also, along with Pete's gold fraternity ring and several beautiful gold necklaces and bracelets he'd given me as gifts over the years. I would have been crushed to lose any of those things.

Next I dug through the drawers of the armoire and through my inexpensive everyday jewelry. Nothing seemed disturbed, except ... except for the brown-hinged box with the white satin lining. My mother's good pearls. Gone. I rummaged further through the shelving and drawers, and the box simply wasn't there. How could I have overlooked the pearls and neglected to hide them as well?

"Pete! Pete—you've got to get up here!"

I examined the window and saw that the narrow dowel I'd placed in the tracks on the sill had snapped. Pieces of it were scattered all over the floor. The dowel wasn't exactly a dowel; it was two wooden chopsticks laid end to end. And they weren't in the window for security reasons—I'd put them there to keep the *bats* out. Pete and I had taken the screens off the windows and left them ajar so our feline menagerie could wade in and out of the house without waking us up in the middle of the night. However, the cats tended to push the windows wide-open. When the neighborhood bats discovered the opening and began flying into the house, we secured the window with these makeshift dowels, leaving an opening that was just cat width but not bat width.

Annie had clearly come in from the roof. There was a spot off our back deck with a piece of fencing that reached up close to the roofline. Whenever Annie or Jeff got locked out of the house, they would jump onto the top of the fence and then climb over onto the roof. One of the windows was always ajar because of the cats. That day, despite the chopstick dowels, Annie had been able to force the window open wide enough to climb inside.

When Pete reached the bedroom, we both stared in disbelief at what was before us. Our own daughter had broken into our family home and stolen from us. Hadn't we already given her everything?

Pete and I continued to check every nook and cranny of the bedroom, including the walk-in closet. There we kept a few gold rings and watches that had been in the family for years, all in one box on the top shelf. I hadn't thought to hide them, and they were now gone. Tina's gold wedding band was among the missing—Tina, the great-grandmother after whom Annie received her middle name, Christina. Pete's tin of loose change and small bills was also gone—the "walking around" money he stashed away for vacations.

After completing our search of the bedroom, we surveyed the rest of the house. Nothing else seemed to be missing. TVs and computers were in place, as were all the silver and everything else of monetary value that was portable. Another thief would have taken more, and the house would have been ransacked. It must have been Annie. The thief who had entered our home knew exactly what she wanted and where to look.

With the damage assessed and our troubled hearts pounding, Pete and I steeled ourselves for a decision. We had recently attended some meetings of a newly launched meth support group, and it was stressed that we must hold our children accountable for their actions, whatever the consequences might be. The group also talked about the potential benefits of using the criminal justice system as a means of intervention.

"Don't treat your children's illegal actions any differently than you would a stranger's," we were told. "Don't interfere with the natural consequences of their actions."

Pete and I gave each other confirming nods, and I took in a calming breath as I reached for the phone and dialed 911.

Calling the police on your own child is not only counterintuitive; it feels like treason. Parenting is all about nurturing, guiding, and protecting—and about keeping your kid *out* of trouble. Family is supposed to be the safe harbor from the storms of life, but that day our family had been violated. We had a right to the sanctity of our own home, to not be held hostage by the outrageous behavior of an addict—even if that addict was one of us. We couldn't control Annie's choices, but we could certainly control our own.

In those decisive moments, it was a sense of purpose that fueled my actions more than anything. Here was an opportunity to act, to intervene. Calculating though it may sound, I welcomed it. The betrayal I felt was immense, but it was secondary to the task at hand. Pete and I knew we had to embrace every possible opportunity to disable our daughter's drug use. We believed the longer Annie stayed on the street, and the deeper she plummeted into her addiction, the lesser the chances of her ever climbing out of that pit. We were determined that jail was better than dead. The prospect of her facing a future with a felony record was not even a consideration that day. As far as we were concerned, Annie didn't have a future.

While waiting for the police to arrive, I called Annette, a friend and former neighbor who owned a high-end fine jewelry store in town. I asked her for an appraisal of my mom's pearls, which we'd need for the police report.

Annie had grown up with Annette's two daughters, and our families had more than a decade of shared history. With years of running back and forth for playtime, parties, or borrowed condiments—heck, I'd even borrowed a cup of bourbon once—we'd forged a permanent path in the brush between our two houses. Although their family was no longer in the neighborhood, I knew they grieved for us, and for Annie too.

My dad had shown me the pearls the day before he gave them to Mom, a gift for their wedding anniversary. He was proud of them, and I could tell they were an expensive strand. Without actually seeing the pearls, Annette could only guess at their value, and she gave me a guesstimate of about $2,500. I suspected that could mean trouble for Annie. I remembered hearing somewhere that the dollar value of a theft has something to do with the charges that are brought in a case.

I'll never forget what Annette said to me.

"You know, Barb, what better use of your mother's pearls than for this purpose? Maybe they'll help bring Annie home." Her comment seemed providential, even at the time.

When the sheriff's deputy finally arrived, Pete and I walked him through the bedroom and the rest of the house. He took pictures and made notes for the police report. We also walked him out to the back deck to show him where Annie had undoubtedly scaled the back fence to get onto the roof. There on the ground, at the foot of the fence, was a half-smoked Marlboro. It was Annie's brand, and I nearly laughed. I could picture her initiating the climb up the fence, hesitating midway to drop her cigarette onto the dirt, freeing both hands. Maybe she would have thought better of leaving the cigarette at the scene of her crime if she'd left the house the same way she entered, but she'd apparently exited through the front door. That explained the unlocked dead bolt.

"Are you sure your daughter didn't use a key to enter the house?" The deputy was trying to determine if this was a true burglary.

"I'm sure," I said. "We asked her to move out about eight

months ago, and I collected her house key then. She's using meth now—ugh, it still sounds so weird to say that. Anyway, we've kind of been expecting this."

"Do you want to press charges?"

"You bet we do," I said without thinking. The immensity of the situation hit me, and the pain I'd been suppressing swelled. My hand came up to my mouth to contain the torrent, but the storm inside me broke loose.

"If it makes you feel any better, ma'am, your daughter didn't do this—drugs did. Meth turns people into criminals real quick."

He was right. It did make me feel better. Not much, but a little.

• • •

A few days later, I received a phone call from a Bend police officer calling from the street. He'd just pulled Annie over on a traffic stop and apparently had reasonable cause to search her car.

"Mrs. Stoefen, your daughter Anna here has some jewelry in her possession. There's a string of pearls and several gold pieces, all in tiny baggies. She tells me she inherited the pearls. Is that true?"

"Well, that would eventually have been true, but I reported the pearls stolen a few days ago. My daughter has a drug problem, and we were pretty sure she'd taken them. There should be a police report on file."

"A report on file? Guess I'll be taking Anna into custody then. The jewelry will be held in evidence for a time, but you'll be able to claim it later at the police station."

Annie was apparently matrixed at the jail again and released almost immediately. She called a few days later.

"What kind of parents have their own daughter arrested?" she demanded.

"You're asking the wrong question, Annie. The real question is, *What kind of daughter steals from her own family?*"

"I just wanted to get back at you for hiding my car. I was high out of my mind, and I guess I went a little nuts."

"Yeah, just a little."

"I was going to return everything eventually."

. . .

Many weeks later, I stomped through the dry fall leaves that lit-
tered the lawn in front of the old Deschutes County courthouse
and climbed the gray stairs to the second floor. All eyes were on
me as I entered the small, somewhat darkened room. The young
deputy district attorney invited me to take a seat. It struck me as
odd that desks and chairs were scattered randomly throughout the
room without the sense of order one might expect from a grand
jury assembly.

When the questioning began, a compassionate woman juror
seated to my left handed me tissues as I testified against Annie.
Through the fog of my tears I scanned the jurors' faces and read
empathy in their expressions. I imagined them wondering what
it must take for a mother to testify against her own child. Had
someone asked me, I would have told them. *It was the only way I
knew to save her.*

# CHAPTER 9

# Despair

How do I write a broken heart? Where are the words to describe the immensity of my loss? My daughter was alive, but she was no longer of this world. She'd slipped through a portal into another dimension, a dark abyss, far from the world in which I lived. Even on the rare occasions when I saw her, the girl into whom I'd poured a lifetime of mother's love no longer inhabited the body I'd brought into the world. Meth had devoured her, and in her flesh now resided a ghastly stand-in, a hollow stranger.

I ached for my daughter. How was I to go forward with this gaping hole in my soul? And why should I want to?

"Annie, come back to me," I whispered from my bed at night.

What a waste. What an abomination. Gone were my dreams for her. Gone were her dreams for herself. Annie was missing her life.

Every corner I turned in our family home, I saw Annie. Family photographs decorated the walls and bookshelves; one in particular inflicted a sickening jab each time I came upon it. It was Annie's high school senior portrait, a lovely vision of her in pink, draped over the low-hanging limb of a tree down by the Deschutes River. It was a painful reminder of all that had been and was now lost. For self-preservation, I removed the portrait from the wall and tucked it inside the hall linen closet. Several other photographs of Annie soon joined it there.

• • •

There were mornings when I continuously played the CD *The Best of Bobby Darin*. Darin was a smash hit in the late fifties, when I was too young to notice, but many of his recordings, like "Mack the Knife" and "Beyond the Sea," have become classics. I developed a morbid fascination with one of his lesser-known titles, "Artificial Flowers." I created metaphors between the Annie in the song and my own Annie, and between artificial flowers and drugs. The song was the perfect companion for my despairing grief.

The words sickened Pete, and he refused to listen, so I blasted the music loudly whenever he was away from the house. Bobby's words gave a voice to my suffering. The pain poured out of me as he sang:

> *Throw away those artificial flowers*
> *Those dumb-dumb flowers*
> *Fashioned from Annie's*
> *Fashioned from A-a-a-annie's des-pa-a-a-air*

I imagined this as the opening song at Annie's funeral, the event I planned every night as I drifted off to sleep. In my mind's eye, I envisioned a sanctuary full of people when "Artificial Flowers" came on over the sound system. Those in attendance would be able to follow the lyrics in the program they'd received at the door, the cover of which was that portrait of Annie I'd hidden in the closet. Pastor Scott would then say a prayer, followed by Annie's high school jazz choir having reassembled to sing "Somewhere Over the Rainbow" in her honor. Next, my dear friend Cheryl would read for me the eulogy I'd prepared. "We lost the fight," it would say.

Late in the service, the big beast who had first given Annie meth would make a surprise appearance, shaking things up by publicly asking for my forgiveness. In my fantasy, I sometimes nobly forgave him and we embraced; yet other times I cursed his life and ordered the police sergeant, who was a member of our church, to take him away.

The service would end with photographs of Annie's life scrolling across the big screen behind the altar, while her longtime best friend and sometimes nemesis, Briana, sang their favorite song from *The Phantom of the Opera*. I hoped Annie would forgive me for asking Briana to sing: "Think of me, think of me fondly, when we've said good-bye."

The sanctuary would then empty as each person placed a long-stemmed white rose either on Annie's casket or by the urn containing her ashes. I never could decide which it should be.

• • •

One morning after Jeff left for school and Pete departed for our office downtown, I lagged behind. I wanted to be alone with Annie for a few minutes.

I reached into the drawer of our entertainment center for a familiar videotape. Flickers of sunlight slipped through the blinds of our rec room until I pulled the shades shut. I inserted the videotape into our player, wrapped myself in a blanket, and curled onto the couch.

Part of the enigma of Annie was her passion for singing in spite of a debilitating problem with stage fright. She could rehearse a song beautifully, but once she was in front of an audience, fear overtook her. The paradox of wanting to perform but not be seen crippled her. Annie's throat would tighten and her voice weaken. This happened time and again at choir performances in high school, at solo ensemble festivals, and at college auditions and recitals. But Annie loved to sing, and she kept putting herself out there.

There was one performance, however, when fear was not the winner. It was a recital arranged by Annie's longtime voice teacher when Annie was nineteen and a sophomore at the community college.

I'd watched this video countless times, yet I still trembled with Annie when her lovely silhouette appeared on the TV screen, standing center stage next to a black grand piano. She wore slim black dress slacks and a fitted black-and-white striped sweater. Her brown hair was long and straight, falling forward across her shoulders.

Annie clasped her hands in front of her, but her twitching fingers betrayed her nervousness as she launched into the opening lines of a Puccini aria:

> *O mio babbino caro,*
> *mi piace, è bello bello.*
> *Oh my dear father,*
> *I like him, he is handsome, handsome.*

The song was about a young Italian girl begging her father for permission to marry the boy she loved. Annie's soprano voice soared higher, the exquisite artistry in the music for once allowing her to forget the audience, to put aside fear and doubt and fully express her passion. The sound flowed out of her as if she'd been born to sing:

> *Si, si, ci voglio andare!*
> *Yes, yes, I want to go there!*

Yet as always, I gripped my blanket harder as she approached the song's climax. Could she reach the high notes this time too? Would she finish strong?

> *E se l'amassi indarno,*
> *andrei sul Ponte Vecchio*
> *ma per buttarmi in Arno!*
> *And if my love were in vain,*
> *I would go to Ponte Vecchio*
> *and throw myself in the Arno!*

Annie sang, her voice both enchanting and anguished.

> *Mi struggo e mi tormento,*
> *O Dio! Vorrei morir!*
> *I am pining and I am tormented,*
> *Oh God! I would want to die!*

The notes floated through the concert hall as if on a cloud.

> *Babbo, pietà, pietà!*
> *Daddy, have mercy, have mercy!*

The distress and pleading in Annie's voice was too much—I both loved it and couldn't bear it. The sound that came from my own voice in response was no lyrical melody. Instead, it was part scream, part guttural groan:

*Aaaaahhhhhhhhhhhhhhhhhhhhh!*

I sat alone in the dark, and the adoring applause on the video-tape mocked my wrenching sobs.

# PART TWO

*There are things that we don't want to happen
but have to accept,
things we don't want to know
but have to learn,
and people we can't live without
but have to let go.*

➤•◄

# CHAPTER 10

# A New Way
# of Thinking

My sister-in-law, Robin, picked up a flyer at her bank in downtown Bend about a support group that was forming for the families of meth addicts. Finally, the prospect of some help!

The first meeting was in a large conference room at a local hospital, and both Pete and I attended. The room was packed, absolutely overflowing with professionals representing all aspects of the treatment and recovery community. And there were frightened parents—lots of them—just as Pete and I were frightened.

Kathie, a nurse at the hospital and the mother of a recovering meth addict, had launched the group. She was passionate about creating a community resource that hadn't been available when her family first found itself in the tailspin of addiction. Pooling the resources of many, we had a burgeoning support system. We called ourselves the Meth Friends and Family Support Group (MFFSG).

The information provided each week was akin to learning a new language. We were taught about addiction, mental health, why addicts use, how they think, how they talk, how they become criminals, and the judicial system that manages them. There were guest speakers from the district attorney's office, the mental health department, the sheriff's office, the police department, and adult parole and probation. We also heard from a dentist who talked about "meth mouth," a nurse practitioner who worked at the jail, and therapists who treated addicts.

It was discouraging to hear law enforcement's take on the meth epidemic, but who could blame them? They saw the revolving door of addicts in and out of the jail, and from their perspective, no one gets better. In fact, one officer told us just that.

"No one really comes back from meth," he said.

One night, however, a therapist from our county mental health services came to our meeting. Many of her clients were mandated by the court to receive therapy, and she carried a large caseload of addicts. I will forever remember her encouragement.

"Don't give up," she told us. "Some addicts do recover. It does happen."

The most compelling speakers, however, were addicts themselves. Several times, Kathie arranged for a panel of recovering addicts to tell their stories, and one night her daughter spoke.

"Hi, my name's Michelle, and I'm a recovering meth addict. I started using drugs when I was thirteen. By the time I was seventeen I was shooting up meth and living on the streets of Bend. I stole from my family and stole from my friends to support my habit. I've been beaten and raped. I've picked through dumpsters for food and slept in the park when I had nowhere to go, using a playground slide as the roof over my head. I've sold myself for bags of dope, and for all the terrible things that have been done to me, I have done to others. I'm in recovery now, but I still struggle from depression and some long-term effects from using."

Michelle was as intense as her story, and she captivated me. Tall and fair, Michelle's perfect grooming presented a striking contrast to the mug shot posted behind her. She was nearly Annie's age, and I wanted to look as deeply into her life as she'd allow.

"My mom had me arrested for stealing her purse. I'd come to the house for my sister's birthday party, but when I saw the purse on the entry table, I grabbed it and ran. The cops later caught me trying to use one of Mom's credit cards."

"How'd you get clean?" I asked. I needed to know how she did it. Was there a "bottom," and if so, what was it? What was the key for getting out, and where could I get one for Annie?

"Everyone's bottom is different," Michelle said. "I had just become so broken, so pathetic. I knew I'd die or be killed if I didn't do something." I turned to look at Kathie to see how she was reacting to what her daughter was saying, and I could see in her expression the relief that her nightmare was now over. I so wanted to be Kathie.

"That last time in jail I decided I'd had enough," Michelle said. "I was so sick and tired of being sick and tired. My mom mailed a list to me in jail of Oregon treatment programs, and I started writing to them. I learned it was possible for people without money to qualify for federal aid, so I got myself on waiting lists. They kept me in jail until one of those beds became available, and then I was released. Treatment took about three months, and then I was in a sober house for several months after that."

As I listened to Michelle, a new dream was born in my heart. Maybe one day Annie would be seated on a recovery panel right beside her.

I sometimes teared up when listening to other recovery presenters share their stories of addiction with our group. One night a young woman with heavy black eyeliner and bright pink streaks decorating her long, ebony hair commented on my obvious distress.

"I never knew there was so much pain on your side of it. I thought we were the only ones who suffered."

It had never occurred to me that Annie might be suffering. On the rare occasions when I saw her, although she looked terrible, she always told me she was "happy." I'd just assumed her life was one perpetual party, a chronic high. But I had no idea where she was living or with whom. Was Annie sleeping in the park like Michelle had? Even in a warm bed she'd always been cold. Was anyone hurting her? Was she as miserable as I was?

• • •

I came to admire the people in recovery. There was something different about them. So many of us go about our lives in relative oblivion and don't make changes, even when we need to—and often not even then. But these addicts were people who needed to change. They had seen the gates of hell and come back not only to tell about it but to flourish as well. I found humility and purpose in their lives. I found ... beauty.

It was addicts who taught me that part of what perpetuates drug use, in addition to the addiction itself, is the desire to numb not only the suffering but also the shame. Might Annie be staying away from the family because of her shame, afraid to take a sober look at the wreckage behind her? I was told that in the stark light of day, the surest cure for virtually every unwelcome emotion is simply more drugs.

Pete and I derived immense support from the group itself. The second half of our meetings was always devoted to personal sharing. We moved our chairs into a circle, each of us taking a turn to talk. We shared heartbreak; we shared hope.

"Jake showed up at home again last night, high," one mother reported, "and he demanded money. He's so abusive when he's using, and it scares me. What happened to my sweet boy? I just can't get him to talk to me anymore, or listen to reason. Where is this all going to end?"

"I know what you mean," another mom said. "My daughter's been using for twelve years now, and my husband and I are raising two of her children. She used to come around every now and then to see the kids, but all it did was upset them. She's so far gone now that I just don't know what's going to happen."

The woman's voice grew somber, and she leaned forward, fixing her eyes on the group. "I actually saw her the other day. This skinny little thing in sweats came shuffling up to me at the grocery store. With her head down and the hood of her sweatshirt pulled forward, she looked so weak and fragile. I thought it was some old lady and didn't realize it was my own Mandy until she looked up at me." She lowered her eyes to the floor as she continued. "We didn't say a word. Mandy just put her arms around me, and we hugged for a moment. Then she was gone."

It wasn't long afterward that we learned the woman's daughter had been arrested on distribution charges and sentenced to five years in prison. While devastating, that turn of events gave the family hope that Mandy might live.

The members of our group represented every walk of life. They were rich and poor, young and old, health care providers, politicians, law officers, homemakers, service workers, business owners, and truck drivers. Our children ranged in age from teens to fortysomething, and as we got to know one another better, we came to the startling realization that all of our children knew each other too. It seems meth was more than a drug; it was also a way of life. In a mostly nocturnal culture, users networked at night in Bend's underbelly—buying and selling from each other, stealing, running, and gunning.

* * *

Outside of our meetings, I continued to search out treatment providers and therapists who specialized in addiction. One day as I made a second round through the Yellow Pages, I stumbled upon a treatment counselor who had time to talk. I told this man about how I'd been chasing after Annie and trying to get her to stop using drugs. He stopped me cold.

"You need to quit doing this to yourself, lady. You need to get out of the way."

I was stunned. "What do you mean *get out of the way*? I'm her mother. She needs me to help her."

"Is what you're doing working?" he asked.

"Not even a little bit," I confessed.

As the counselor's words sank in, it was a pivotal aha moment for me. Counterintuitive for a parent, for sure, the concept lined up with much of what I was learning in group. Chasing after Annie just gave her more power, and it was making me nuts, possibly even sick.

"No one stays in addiction without help," he said to me. "Parents want so much to fix things. We give the wrong kind of help and unwittingly further enable our kids to continue their destructive behaviors. But be ready with a plan. Someday she may reach out and ask for real help. When she does, you may have only a small window of time in which to act."

So in our group, we learned not to help. That is, we stopped our enabling behaviors. We didn't bail our children out of jail, hire attorneys, give them money, give them rides, or pay their bills. And there was no rescuing unless doing so involved a ride for medical treatment or to rehab.

It wasn't easy learning to distinguish enabling from offering real help. It took time, and trial and error. And sometimes it took courage. Watching the people we loved take their falls was both scary and painful, and in the absence of a crystal ball, we never knew how circumstances would play out.

While there was no guarantee the changes we made would lead to any discernible behavioral changes in our children, it was crazy-weird how it sometimes did. Over a period of time, several of the addicts represented in the group entered into sustained recovery.

At a friend's suggestion, I also at this time began attending Al-Anon meetings. Al-Anon is a recovery community technically for the families of alcoholics, but other drug addictions are often represented by its members as well. While it is nonreligious, one can apply the tenets of one's own faith, or even unfaith, to the program's spiritual principles.

Most people enter Al-Anon with the misconception that it is where we learn to get our loved one to stop drinking or using drugs. I was no different. What I was surprised to discover, however, was that this twelve-step program isn't about the addict at all; it's about us.

In Al-Anon I began a daily process of reading and reflection, and a door was opened for me into a new way of thinking. These new ideas blew into my life like a fresh breeze, clearing the haze and unburying truths that resonated deeply:

- We can't change others; we can only change ourselves.
- It's not up to me.
- When we change the way we look at things, the things we look at change.*
- If we keep doing what we've always done, we'll keep getting what we've always gotten.†
- We're not responsible for the choices of another, not even the people we raised.

Through Al-Anon I explored my codependency with Annie. I came to understand what Karen had meant when she'd said, "Maybe Annie has been loved too much." At the time of Annie's first depression, I really glommed onto her and became somewhat addicted, or codependent, to all of her life issues. My intentions were good. I wanted—needed—to keep my shy, depressed, and insecure child safe. Appointing myself Annie's life manager seemed an obvious solution. But we became too close. Even Jeff saw it. When he started high school, he sat me down and said, "Just so ya know, Mom, I'm not going to be telling you everything the way Annie does."

The principles of Al-Anon helped me realize that unless I set Annie free, she would never find her own way. My codependency had by no means caused her addiction, but in some ways it may have kept her stuck.

At that time I also began to look at Annie differently. It finally dawned on me that her drug use wasn't something she was *doing* to her family—it, in fact, had nothing to do with us. I was able to stop thinking about her addiction in terms of fault, hers or mine. I'm grateful not to have stayed in the torment of self-blame for long. I certainly could have after learning Annie first tried meth

---

*This principle is attributed to Dr. Wayne Dyer.
†This principle is often attributed to W. L. Bateman.

just weeks after we'd asked her to leave the family home. But I knew then, as I do now, if it hadn't been meth, it would have been something else.

She had been an adult and living her own life, such as it was, so I was not responsible for Annie's choices any more than she was responsible for mine. And I wasn't responsible for her addiction any more than I was for the size of her feet.

To quote an Al-Anon slogan, "I didn't cause it; I can't control it; I can't cure it."

It wasn't my fault.

# CHAPTER 11

# Let Go
# and Let God

When my daughter fell into meth addiction at the age of twenty-two, the faith that I had built—in fact, all I'd come to believe—was called into question. I was furious with God.

I'd been a faithful Christian. I was a good mother. I took my kids to church. I took the neighbor kids to church. I volunteered in Sunday school. I read my Bible. I honored God. I didn't swear (much). I gave money to the homeless. I wrote checks, cooked meals, and cleaned homes for those in need. And I was hyper-vigilant about the integrity of my business practices. I did everything except put a fish decal on my car, lest my husband drive it and give someone a questionable gesture for cutting him off.

The outrage I felt at God for allowing meth to take my daughter was second only to the agony I felt in losing her. I often slipped into the garage at night, away from Pete and Jeff, to vent and rage and scream at God.

Between outbursts, I'd relight the butt of a cigarette I'd saved in a drawer by the door and take a couple of hits until I was too dizzy to continue. I'd quit smoking twenty years before, and it was utter insanity to be opening that door again, but I didn't care. Hurting myself felt strangely comforting. Maybe it was my own form of cutting, as Annie had done. It was almost like biblical times, when widows beat themselves or put hot ashes on their heads. These were my hot ashes, a manifestation of my grief.

I didn't want to buy a whole pack of cigarettes and risk a total smoking relapse, so I frequented a nearby market that sold individual cigarettes for a quarter. While there, I'd glare at the ornate glass pipes on display next to the register and fantasize about the glass flying after a few wild flings of my purse. I once commented to the young sales clerk about them.

"I'm surprised the DA allows you to sell that drug paraphernalia."

"Oh, people buy these for smoking tobacco," he said.

"Yeah right they do." I made certain my sarcasm wasn't lost on him. "I started smoking before you were born, and I've never seen tobacco in one of those things."

He shrugged and handed me the two cigarettes I'd just purchased for fifty cents. I wanted so much to boycott that market because of all the wasted lives represented by those vile glass pipes, but it was the only store in town that sold individual cigarettes, and I needed my ashes.

I continued to meet with God in the garage over a period of weeks. I stood at the bottom of the few stairs that led into the mudroom inside the house, lighting and relighting my cigarette butts, praying aloud and raging at God.

*"Dear God, please, please help me. Help Annie. Save her—please. I beg you. Do you hear me, God? How could you let this happen? I did everything I was supposed to do. I loved you. You promised—what am I supposed to do now? Just tell me what to do ..."*

I sometimes felt guilty about my rants, not because I thought God couldn't take it, but because I wasn't quite sure I was worthy of his attention. I knew he was busy. The war in Iraq was in full swing, and the death count climbed daily. Both American and Iraqi women were losing their children. There were kidnappings, with stories of gruesome beheadings, and all I could think was, *Each of these victims has a mother.* How much greater was her suffering than mine, that her child should die this terrifying, torturous death. And to know it was videotaped as it happened.

My heart started to open to this kind of suffering. Feelings of "why me?" began to give way to "why not me?"

One Sunday my friend Suzanne and I stood in the back of the church during worship, commiserating over the dire state of both our daughters' lives.

"Well, that's life," she said.

*That's life.* One of those throwaway lines everyone uses. But I heard it with new understanding that morning.

"Is it? Is that life?" I asked her.

She wasn't saying to me, "That's life; get over it" or "That's life; that's what all the people say." She was saying, "Life's hard." Really, really hard.

I had lived too long to carry the belief that if life was hard, something was terribly wrong. Had my life really been that easy, or was I simply that clueless?

Later that night, after dinner, I slipped away again to the garage for another smoke. The guys were watching *Sunday Night Football.* They wouldn't miss or hear me, though I knew I'd catch heck from both of them when I returned smelling of cigarettes.

I exited the house through the mudroom door and walked down the steps, and with both cars still in the driveway, I stared into the empty expanse of the garage. *God, are you here? I so need you to be here.*

I dropped to the floor, wincing when my left knee connected with the unforgiving concrete. I lowered myself into a prayerful position, shivering on the cold floor. It was literally freezing in the garage.

I eyed the raised veins on the back of my hands as they lay flat against my thighs, then slowly raised my palms to my face and began to pray. There I spilled my burden and my tears before the throne of God.

*I need you. I need you in the worst way. Jesus. Please. Meet me here.* I shifted my position to relieve the throbbing in my knee and wiped my nose with the sleeve of my Oregon sweatshirt.

*Help me. Jesus, help me. How do I go forward with this hole in my soul? Why was Annie even born, only to be lost in this way? What possible sense am I to make of this?*

I'd come to the end of myself. *"I'm begging you, God. What am I to do? Just tell me what to do!*

At the end of this desperate cry, cutting through the emotional mist in my brain, I felt an answer well up from deep inside me.

"Give her to me."

*Huh?*

"Give her to me."

This must seem nonsensical to people who don't talk to God. It frankly sounds so to me as I write it. But that was my experience. In his book *The Shack*, William P. Young describes it as "hearing the voice within my own." He explains it perfectly. It was familiar, but it wasn't my voice. It was the steady, all-knowing, authoritative speaker I'd rarely heard before, and only when quiet enough to discern it.

I hesitate to even talk about those moments in the garage because of the credibility it could cost me. *I* might not even believe me. I've looked askance at some who claimed to hear God and sometimes deemed it wishful thinking, if not complete arrogance. But maybe I'd been selling God short. Maybe he does sometimes speak to the simplest of hearts. Even hearts like mine.

"Give her to me" is what God said in the garage that night. And so, with the greatest leap of faith I have ever known, I handed over my most precious girl to my invisible God—because he'd said so. I think I even extended my arms into the room to complete the spiritual transaction, making the transfer from my care to his.

I was blinded by a further release of tears produced in the intensity of that moment—tears of exhaustion, sadness, fear, as well as tears of profound joy. I swelled with awe, knowing that the creator of the universe loved me, and Annie, enough to show up in my garage and take over.

Annie was now in God's hands. I felt I could breathe again. I didn't know where she was, but he did. And while I fully understood that God was not a vending machine where you drop in a prayer and out pops a blessing, I knew that nothing was impossible for him. I didn't know if he *would* save her, but I knew that he was able.

In the ensuing weeks, once I stopped telling God what to do and how to do it, that last modicum of control ultimately gave way to a prayer I prayed all day, every day, forty-two times a day, for nearly a year:

*"Lord, wherever Annie is today, please protect her. Please free her from this bondage, and lead her into the life you created her for."*

• • •

Why is there suffering in the world? The most honest and complete answer I have to that question is, "I don't know." But I do know that God is near, and he's in the battle with me.

CHAPTER 12

# Courtroom
# Intervention

Annie made a surprise appearance at our office on the morning of her first court appearance. Arriving early, she made a bed out of the plaid wing chair and ottoman until it was time to leave. Given the charges she was facing, I was perplexed to see her. I couldn't tell if she was after moral support or a place to crash, but at the appointed time we three drove over to the courthouse together. What Annie didn't know is that I'd already negotiated a deal with the district attorney's office, and instead of more jail time, Pete and I would take her to treatment that very day. Out of view and under blankets in the back of our Expedition was a bag for her, already packed.

While Annie had never expressed interest in or willingness to go to treatment, several treatment counselors I'd consulted insisted it could be beneficial even if someone is admitted against his or her will.

"It can still work; the miracles can still happen," I was told. I sure hoped so. I was willing to try just about anything to rid my daughter's life of drugs. I'd even fantasized with my brother, Paul, about having Annie kidnapped and "deprogrammed," like parents of the Moonies used to do in the seventies. She sure acted like someone who'd been brainwashed. I imagined having her abducted and taken to a remote location out in the desert, and locked in an old warehouse from which there was no escape. She'd be well cared for and denied drugs and alcohol until she came to her senses. We could then all go home together and live happily ever after once again.

If I'd thought kidnapping Annie would have solved the problem, I'd have done it. I would have shot her in the foot to save her.

Once we arrived in the courtroom and Annie's name was called, she joined the public defender up in front while the judge read the charges against her: two counts of possession of a controlled substance and one count of burglary I. The burglary charge was for my mother's pearls.

I watched Annie as the judge reviewed the charges. Her back stiffened. Seems she was just learning that Pete and I had pressed charges for breaking into our house. When ordered to treatment, she shook her head as if to say "no way," and then she protested to her attorney when it was revealed her dad and I would be taking her. After some serious-looking counsel, however, Annie reluctantly agreed. If I had to guess, she was told it was either treatment or jail—or worse.

Annie was furious, and her reaction made me question whether Pete and I had done the right thing. It troubled me to ambush her like that, and in spite of all we'd been through, I hated having her so mad at me. But Pete and I had to stop her if we could. There were hard choices to be made.

Annie sat silently in the back of our car for the ride out of town, sniffing incessantly and dabbing at her runny nose.

"Do you have a cold?" I asked.

"No," was all she offered. I then remembered her trip to the bathroom just minutes before we entered the courtroom, and now wondered if she may have snorted something. That seemed like something an addict might want to do before facing a judge.

I'd called ahead to the treatment center, and when we arrived, an intake coordinator was waiting for us. She ushered Annie inside while Pete and I lingered in the doorway, not quite knowing what to do with ourselves. This was new territory. We knew nothing about rehab protocol.

Annie's vitals were taken, and she was weighed in at 103 pounds. She was downright frail for her nearly five-foot-eight-inch frame, and down thirty pounds from where I last remembered her. There wasn't a curve left on her body. My daughter now had what looked to be the body of a twelve-year-old boy.

I studied Annie as she moved across the room to take a chair and answer a list of intake questions. Her once luxurious mane of sun-streaked, elbow-length brown hair was now cropped and thinning, revealing bits of gray-colored scalp beneath. She wore a tank top and a pair of cargo pants I'd never seen before. Nothing about my daughter seemed familiar. She even smelled different. I was grateful there were no track marks on her arms — at least she hadn't graduated to using needles. Maybe there was a silver lining to her longtime fear of shots and blood tests.

Annie would spend her first few days of treatment in detox, being observed for signs of withdrawal. We were told that most amphetamine addicts don't have physical withdrawal, and they typically just crash and sleep for days. It's never known, however, if heroin or other opiates are also present in someone's system, making withdrawal intense or painful — and potentially dangerous. Once she was deemed safe, Annie would then move into the main house, joining thirteen other residents already in the treatment program.

Pete went to the car and brought in the bag I'd packed for Annie, along with the bedding we'd been told to bring. There was a white blanket with white satin trim, a pillow, and a set of twin sheets I'd bought for camp when she was fifteen. They were crisp, blue-and-white checked cotton percale. So fresh and feminine, and the sight of them made me heartsick. I loved those sheets, and even though we no longer had twin beds in our house, I'd saved them in case Annie ever had a little girl of her own. But marriage and a family seemed a near impossibility for my daughter on that day.

Pete and I prepared to leave. "I love you, Annie," I told her. She rebuffed my attempt at a hug, so we stiffly made our exit. My expression must have betrayed my fear. The intake coordinator provided some comfort as she showed us to the door.

"I know how hard this is," she said. "But you're doing the right thing."

I forced a weak smile. "Thanks. I really needed to hear that."

We had little contact with Annie over the next couple of weeks, but reports from her case manager were encouraging. Annie had engaged, she was following the rules, and she was working a program of recovery — at least as far as anyone could tell. In fact, my daughter was reportedly a model client. In my mind, this, frankly, didn't add up. I'd felt sure she would put up a fight — rehab couldn't possibly be this easy. But maybe, just maybe, our nightmare was finally over. I was giddy at the prospect.

At the end of the third week, Annie was offered the privilege of coming home for the weekend. Pete and I picked her up from the treatment center on a Friday afternoon. Before heading home, we met with both Annie and her counselor to discuss the rules for the weekend. We also toured the facility and met some of Annie's compatriots in the program, one of whom was named Taylor. The moment I spotted him on the deck outside the mess hall, I was certain we'd be hearing about this guy. Taylor looked to be in his late twenties, and with wavy, sandy brown hair and tanned, rugged good looks, I knew he'd be of interest to Annie. She had the uncanny ability to always capture the attention of the best-looking guy in any situation, apparently even in rehab.

When Annie walked across the threshold of our family home that warm October afternoon, drug free, it was a glorious homecoming. Could it be that our prodigal daughter had finally come back to us?

Jeff greeted Annie with his usual reserve, but he did offer a hug. He had missed her. Just shy of six-foot-six, he now towered over Annie, and while five years her junior, most people now thought he was the older sibling. Once those first awkward moments had passed, Jeff picked Annie up and threw her over his shoulder like a sack of grain, just as he had done a zillion times before. Annie predictably squealed with delight, just as she had done a zillion times before. It was heartwarming to see them together again.

We four had a celebratory dinner of homemade mac and cheese—Annie's favorite—and took turns recounting the family's favorite jokes.

Annie began. "What did the bartender say to the horse?"

"Why the long face?" Pete and I chimed together.

Then twisting his mustache, Pete channeled Groucho Marx. "I went hunting and shot a bear in my pajamas. How he got in my pajamas I'll never know."

How is it that the same old, tired jokes still make us laugh? It's the shared history, I guess, some of the glue that bonds us together.

I was about to suggest a movie as we cleared the dinner dishes, but Annie jumped in before I could speak. She stood to announce she was leaving and asked for the keys to her car that had been parked in our driveway while she was in treatment. My heart stopped.

"That's not the plan," I protested. "Aren't you supposed to stay here?"

"I want to go to a twelve-step meeting. You know, one of those anonymous things. It's okay to do that."

"Uh, where's the meeting? How long will you be gone?"

"It's downtown at that old church. I looked it up. The meeting goes seven to eight. I'll be back before eight thirty."

Pete and I wished we could hold Annie hostage that weekend, but a twelve-step meeting was part of her program, and we guessed it was okay. It was a good sign she wanted to go, so I decided to give her the keys to my car, not the keys to hers. And I handed her my cell phone—hers had long been MIA. She'd definitely have to return the car, and we could stay connected with the cell.

"I'll call if I'm late for any reason," she said.

Annie headed out the driveway in my red Explorer, and I was cautiously optimistic. We had a plan in place, and Annie was showing some encouraging new behaviors. We decided to trust her—that is, until the phone rang shortly before 8:30. It was Annie.

"I'm having coffee with a friend, and I'll be back in a little while."

"Is this a friend from your meeting?" I asked.

"I actually didn't make it to the meeting, but this friend is clean. It's okay."

She'd lied to us about going to a meeting. "Annie, this isn't what we agreed to. You need to come home."

"I'm not ready to come home yet. It'll be fine, Mom."

"Your counselor was very specific about the rules. You're not supposed to be out late. Please come home."

"I'm not ready to come home. Leave me alone." She was starting to sound agitated, and I was becoming concerned.

"I don't like the sound of this, Annie. You're breaking our agreement. You really need to come home right now. It's not safe for you to be out on your own right now."

"I'm twenty-two years old. You can't tell me what to do."

It was déjà vu. "I know how old you are, but you're here with special permission this weekend. Come on, Annie ..."

"I'll come home when I'm ready."

"Okay, if you're not here by ten, we're locking the doors and going to bed." The counselor had told us to keep those kinds of boundaries.

"What!" Annie was really getting worked up now. "That really sucks, Mom. You can't do this."

"We made a deal, and you're breaking it. Let me put it to you this way—you no longer have permission to use my car."

"Just watch me." She hung up.

My heart sank about twelve stories. I called Annie several times during the next few hours, and she didn't answer. *Here we go*, I thought. There was no way of telling when we might see her again. I decided to see how things would play out over the weekend before calling the police about my car.

Jeff was disgusted and hurt, so he made an exit and headed over to his girlfriend's house. Pete stayed lodged in front of the TV, soothing himself with a glass of wine, while I locked all the doors and went upstairs to bed. I crawled between the sheets in our darkened room, and the familiar sadness returned and enveloped me once again. I lay in wait for the distant sound of a car coming up our road, hoping and praying for headlights to appear in the driveway. I'd waited for those headlights on hundreds of nights throughout the years, and they'd always faithfully appeared. But I hadn't seen them for nearly a year now.

*Oh, God, is this ever going to end?*

I somehow surrendered to sleep, but didn't much care if morning came or not.

Pete and I heard nothing from Annie until her return on Sunday, two days later. She came into view with my car squealing down our long driveway, halting abruptly near the front steps. She burst through the front door, slammed my keys and cell phone on the kitchen counter, and charged down the hall to her old bedroom in the back of the house. I followed, finding myself chasing after her once again.

Annie wanted nothing to do with me. She was on fast-forward, her neck stiff and jerking, and she was snarling at me like a rabid dog. *High*, I thought. She covered her ears as I tried to reason her into a calmer mood.

"Annie, you can still go back to treatment. This doesn't have to be a deal breaker."

"No way. I'm not going back there."

"Are you high?"

"I wouldn't be if it wasn't for you. You locked me out of the house Friday night. This is all *your* fault."

I decided not to argue with her, recalling advice to not "pick up the rope." In a power struggle the addict will always win. Everything is always someone else's fault.

Annie stuffed into her backpack the few pieces of clothing she'd brought home and demanded the keys to her car. I willingly handed them over. While she may have felt she'd won the battle when I gave her the keys, I'd come to believe that the war could best be won with the car in her possession. Not only had it repeatedly been the source of so much trouble for her, but it would make it easier for the authorities to find her again. I was intent that repeated consequences would wear her down.

With a barrage of profanities, Annie slammed the front door and was gone. I walked straight to the phone and dialed the treatment center, informing the case manager that Annie would not be back. And I told them to keep the blue-checked bedsheets. Maybe another young woman would find comfort in them, and find her way clear of the bondage of drugs.

The next morning I called the district attorney's office. Leaving treatment had been a violation of Annie's probation. I was told a warrant would immediately go out for her arrest.

# CHAPTER 13

# Impossible Days

I awakened one October morning about two weeks later, wondering if I'd hear from Annie. Did she even track the days of the week? With no job to show up for, no bills to pay, and no place to live, she'd have no need to. I guessed she didn't even own a calendar. Nevertheless, her call came that afternoon. I'd just walked in the door after bailing early from work.

"Happy birthday, Mom. See, I remembered. Surprised?" Her tone was flat, but there were traces of Annie in it.

"Yes, I am, actually. Thanks for calling, sweetie. My day is more complete having heard from you. How are you?" A silly question I nevertheless continued to ask.

"I'm very *tired*," she said. "I was wondering if I could come over and spend some birthday time with you and then maybe sleep over?"

So that's why she called. Annie needed a place to crash. "We have plans for dinner tonight," I said, "so I don't think a sleepover will work, but I'd love to see you before then. Can you come over now?"

"Well, see, there's a problem with my car. This guy kind of stole it and now won't give me my keys back. I still have that AAA card, so I had it towed to the dealership where he can't find it. Guess it will have to sit there until I can come up with a hundred and ninety bucks for a new ignition key. I'm over at the Old Mill—can you pick me up here?"

Having the car towed seemed a resourceful solution to her problem. "Okay," I said with some hesitancy. "Once Jeff gets home, he and I will come get you." Based on what I'd learned in our group, I'd begun to consider Annie potentially dangerous and wasn't going to get into a car with her alone. Meth could make people do crazy things, sometimes even to parents.

Jeff walked in the door from school about three o'clock, and after a quick snack, he and I jumped into my car to fetch Annie. He stayed in the car while I entered the jewelry store where she'd asked to meet, but there I saw only the concerned faces of our friends who owned it.

"Annie was here, but she just left," Annette told me. "She looks just awful, Barb. I'm so sorry. Is there anything I can do to help?"

"Pray," I said, starting to tear up. "Do you have any idea where she went?"

"Tasha followed her down the road and was trying to talk some sense into her. They might still be out there."

Just then Tasha walked into the store. "Annie's out there waiting for you, Barb. I told her it didn't have to be like this, and that we're here to help whenever she's ready."

"Thanks, guys. Thanks for everything. I gotta go. I'll see you later."

"Oh, and Barb, happy birthday," Annette said.

"Yeah, thanks. Happy birthday to me."

I walked outside and found Annie about a hundred feet from the store. She grabbed the backpack that was on the ground beside her and made a beeline for the car. I wanted to hug her, but an invisible shield around her said, "Don't touch." She was all business. A flat "hey Jeff" was all she had to say as we got in the car and headed out of the parking lot.

Pete was home when we got there, and the four of us sat on

the couch and made small talk until Annie became supine on her favorite spot. Her cat, Peanut, who was now living with us, was under one arm, wedged between her and the back of the couch, with his head burrowed up into her neck. It was such a familiar sight and should have brought me comfort, but Annie seemed a stranger that day, an intruder in our home.

After an hour or so, I nudged her awake and told her we had to leave. We had dinner reservations at six. Would it be possible for me to say good-bye to Annie without inviting her to join us for my birthday dinner?

"Where can we drop you?" I asked her.

"I don't have anywhere to go, Mom. I just need to sleep. Can't I stay here?"

"I'm sorry, Annie. For obvious reasons, I'm not comfortable leaving you in the house when we're not here. There must be somewhere we can take you. Isn't there a friend's house where you can stay?"

"There's nowhere."

"Well, you've been staying somewhere. Can't you go wherever that is?"

"That's not an option anymore."

I searched my mind for possibilities. "Well, we could drop you off at your car. You still have a door key to get in it, right? You'd be safe in the parking lot at the dealership."

"Sleep in my car?"

"Would it be the first time?" I asked.

Annie was silent.

"Come on," I said. "Let's go."

The four of us drove across town. As we approached the dealership parking lot and the spot where Annie's car was parked, memories came flooding back of the day we'd given it to her. Pete and I had ushered her into the showroom, just steps from where we were now. When she'd spotted a red bow the size of Montana sitting atop the glistening black sedan, she knew it was hers. There were squeals of delight as she hugged the windshield.

Pete pulled up near the side door of Annie's car. She exited obediently.

"Take care of yourself, sweetheart," I said. "I love you."

"K. Bye." Annie stood there and watched us drive away.

Anguished by the unthinkable that had just occurred, Pete, Jeff, and I drove in silence to our family's favorite Italian bistro. There I proceeded to drink myself into oblivion.

• • •

Later that evening, after we'd returned home from dinner, the phone rang. It was Annie calling from a pay phone.

She pleaded with me. "Can't I please stay the night? I just need to sleep. Please ... Mom."

I caved. Not wanting to enable her drug use or be held hostage by her lifestyle, I'd tried so hard to be strong. But I just couldn't say no to her twice in one day. Maybe God was giving me a second chance to be merciful, or maybe I simply succumbed to a persistent addict. Whatever the case, Jeff drove me back to the dealership and we brought Annie home.

Without so much as a good night, she charged down the hall to the back bedroom like a wanderer in the desert who had just spotted water. She hibernated for thirty-six straight hours, rising only once to empty her bladder. Not yet understanding the sleep patterns of a meth addict, I tried several times to rouse her, and even once put a mirror under her nose to check for telltale signs of respiration. At each intrusion, Annie stirred slightly and muttered only the word *sleep*.

Upon awakening the morning of the third day, she nibbled on what she could find in the fridge and then joined me on the couch.

"Ah, I needed that."

"I've never seen anyone sleep like that. Are you all right?"

"Yeah, I'm fine. I'd been up for about a week, maybe even longer, and really needed to crash."

"A week? You were awake for a week?"

"Oh, that's nothing. I've been awake as long as two weeks before. It does make you pretty crazy, though. I did hallucinate some."

"Annie, you need to stop doing this or you are going to *die*. Please let us help you."

Her mood changed instantly. "Just leave me alone. I don't want your help." With that she jumped off the couch and made a bee-line for the phone sitting across the room. Within minutes she'd grabbed her backpack and was out the door, waiting for her ride at the top of the driveway.

I realized we'd given Annie the respite to fuel another run. I felt conned, vowing to never do it again. But Pete and I were making the best decisions we could as each situation presented itself. As much as we tried to plan for every contingency, for each what-if, something would shift, and we'd have to find our footing again. It was a dance we did, stepping to unfamiliar music and a beat that was forever changing.

• • •

I had lunch with Virginia, my dear friend and realtor, later that week. She'd been baptized with Annie and me years before, and we'd felt a sisterhood ever since that day.

"Remember how afterward all of us were dripping wet and giggling and slipping on the bathroom floor when we changed at the church?" I said. "Annie loved every bit of it."

"There will be more great days like that, Barb. You'll see."

"I was so naive, Virginia. I thought if I loved God and did all the right things, Annie would too. Now look at her. She's gone. Completely lost."

"I see greatness in Annie," she said.

I nearly screamed at Virginia. "What are you talking about? Have you heard nothing I've been telling you?"

"Greatness. That's what I see."

• • •

"Pete, can you get that, please?" My office telephone blared for the umpteenth time one morning, and I was already loopy from fielding a barrage of calls. "Pete, are you in there?"

The constant interruption of the phone that day derailed me from pressing work I needed to finish before heading to a doctor's appointment. I'd had some vertigo lately. I felt like I was tipping over.

"Pete!" I picked up the phone on the fourth ring, just before the call went to voice mail. I had the phone in one hand and a tuna sandwich in the other.

"Hi, this is Barb."

Silence.

"Hello ...?"

*"Mom."*

"Annie. What's the matter?"

"Something's happened to Taylor. I don't know what to do."

"Huh? Where are you?" A familiar panic rose inside of me. My heart started to race.

"I just called his house, but his mom answered. The ambulance was there." Through her sobs, I could barely make out what my daughter was saying.

"What? Take a breath, sweetie. I can't understand you. Now, what's going on?"

"I was supposed to meet Tay last night. You know, the guy from treatment. But it got late. I had stuff to do and never got there." Annie's distress escalated. "His mom said the ambulance was there. I asked if he was okay, and all she said was 'No, he's not.' I should have been there."

"So ... he relapsed? I thought he was doing so well."

"I guess his old girlfriend showed up, and she's still using."

"Annie, tell me where you are and I'll come get you."

"Just help me find out if he's okay. I feel like this is all my fault. This wouldn't have happened if I'd been there."

"Annie, it's *not* your fault. You didn't put the needle in his arm. Is there anyone you can call to find out what's going on?"

"I don't know." Annie's voice had faded to a whimper, just like it had done when she was a little girl.

"Just tell me where you are." I was scared for her.

"No."

"Come on. Let me help you."

"It doesn't matter."

"It does matter. Annie, talk to me. Maybe we can call somebody. Where are you?"

"I gotta go."

"Wait. Maybe I can call the sheriff's office. Maybe they can tell us what's happened to Taylor."

"Yeah, let's call the sheriff. Right."

"Annie, I'm just trying to help."

"Forget it. Maybe I'll just drive over there."

"Over where?"

"To Taylor's."

"Will you at least let me know what you find out?"

"Sure." The line went silent.

"Hello? Hello? Annie!"

She was gone.

My heart hammered against my ribs. I'm not sure which was most frightening—the feeling that my heart might literally explode or the surreal quality of the moment. Whatever the case, I took comfort in knowing I'd be seeing my doctor.

Before long I was waiting for her in the exam room, whirling with anxiety. Stretched out on the exam table, I attempted calming breaths, but the feeling that I was levitating only intensified my distress.

I had gone to this doctor for years. Annie had been a patient here too, so it seemed the perfect place for the emotional meltdown I'd been working up to for months. What safer place than a doctor's office should I need resuscitation or someone to grab the back of my shirt to keep me from being sucked through the looking glass and into oblivion?

When the doctor finally entered the room, I sobbed out the

details of Annie's call that morning and the insanity that was now my life. Annie was killing herself with drugs, and I was going down right along with her. All I wanted in that moment was a little compassion. Yet as I unloaded my burden, absolutely drunk with despair, my doctor flitted about the exam room like a giddy teenager before a date. The doctor was more engrossed in finding a wayward stethoscope than in listening to me.

"Oh, yes. There were lots of addicts being treated at the inner-city hospital where I trained." The doctor spoke breathlessly, as if recounting an invigorating ski run that morning up at Mount Bachelor. "Most of them live that way their whole lives."

I was incredulous. Annie wasn't just *some addict*. She was my daughter, and this doctor's patient.

After a thirty-second diagnosis I was handed a prescription and dismissed.

"What about the vertigo?" I asked.

"I'm sure your high blood pressure is causing it."

"But that call from Annie could have—"

"Bye, nice seeing you." The doctor left the exam room in one swift motion and closed the door. I guessed my eight minutes were up.

*Really?*

It was yet another surreal moment in my day. I sobered up quickly, indignant that I'd just exposed my suffering to someone who simply didn't care. I tossed the prescription and never returned.

• • •

Taylor's poor mother—what she must have been going through. I'd never met her, but she did call me once after Taylor completed treatment. He'd been clean for three months, and since Annie wasn't clean, she'd wanted my help in keeping my daughter away from him. She knew Annie could pose a danger to her son's recovery. What Taylor's mom didn't understand, however, was that there was nothing I could do to keep them apart. I didn't even know where Annie was, since she'd bailed from treatment a few weeks earlier. And how would I be able to *make* her do anything anyway?

I'd heard that heroin relapses are the worst. After a period of abstinence, it's easy to overdose when the body has lost its tolerance for the drug. I felt momentarily grateful that Annie was using meth instead of heroin. Meth is the most addictive drug on the planet and will certainly ruin your life before it kills you—but heroin will kill you quicker. There just aren't many old, active heroin addicts.

I didn't hear from Annie again for over a week. When she did call, I asked about Taylor. He had indeed overdosed. He was dead.

# CHAPTER 14

# Jeremiah

It was a bright November afternoon, and I'd just stumbled through the front door with an armload of pinecones when I heard the phone ring. I'd made the dash out into the yard in my bare feet to collect elements for a Thanksgiving table arrangement, stinging my flesh on the frozen ground.

The caller was a woman named Maggie. She lived in a small ranching town in eastern Oregon. Maggie introduced herself as the mother of a young man named Rick who had just driven into town with Annie. Both had been arrested on drug possession charges. Annie and Rick were presently lodged in the Grant County jail, and Maggie had just come from there, having responded to her son's call for help. She was calling to let me know about the arrest and to also let me know that Annie was safe. The mother of a drug addict herself, she knew the relief that came with news of a child's whereabouts.

Maggie explained that her son had apparently been driving Annie's car, and a local police officer on patrol recognized him as someone with an outstanding warrant in his county. When Rick was pulled over, drugs were found in the car, and the car was impounded once again. Annie wasn't in the car at the time of Rick's arrest, but he'd told officers the drugs were hers. When she later showed up at the impound yard to claim the car, the police were waiting for her. Annie was arrested on the spot and taken into custody.

She called home later in the day, fuming.

"This wasn't my fault, Mom. Rick is lying—those weren't my drugs. He does not get to put this all on me."

It was almost comical that Annie thought it mattered whose drugs they were. What difference did it make? Both of them were culpable as far as I was concerned, and it seemed a sure bet she was using them as well. But Annie insisted there were no drugs in the car when they'd left Bend. The road trip had been an attempt to simply get away—she from the trauma of Taylor's death and both of them from the drug scene in general.

Annie told us she was scheduled to be released in two days, and she asked if we could come to town and get the car out of impound for her. She had no resources whatsoever in John Day, where she was in jail and her nearest friend was in jail with her. The fee for the car would be about $200.

"We'll come get you and pay the impound fee on one condition," I told her. "You must agree to go back to treatment. I've been talking to the people at the treatment center again, and they said they'd welcome you back, provided you call your counselor there and work out the details yourself." I knew it was long shot, but I gave it the shot nonetheless. "We'll give you your car back once you successfully complete treatment."

"Okay, well ... maybe. Would you want me to come back to Bend with you right away?"

"Yes, I don't see it working any other way. Your dad can drive our car home, and you and I can come back together in your car."

"All right. I guess I can do that. Yeah, sure. Can you be here day after tomorrow about noon? I'll meet you at the impound yard."

Annie was lying. I knew she had no intention of going to treatment, and I had no intention of giving her the car back unless she did. This was the Camry's third impound, and I wanted it back once and for all. I refused to allow its continued use as a pack wagon for drug addicts, and because it had significant value left in it, Pete and I now planned to sell it. Annie would hate us for it, maybe forever, but it was a risk we needed to take. I hoped that if we ever got on the other side of all this, Annie would one day understand. "We loved you that much," I would tell her.

While we'd once used the Camry as a virtual tracking device and sometimes as a bargaining chip, it now seemed that reclaiming the car was the best tool at our disposal to disable Annie's lifestyle. It would have been ideal to allow those consequences to unfold naturally, without our interference, as they undoubtedly would have in the face of future impounds and incarcerations. However, Pete and I were unwilling to experience those consequences with Annie and see our investment go down the addiction drain.

For several years we'd been dealing with the lying and false promises of an alcoholic, pothead, and now meth addict, and we knew better than to believe Annie would just trot off to treatment. In fact, I was fairly certain she wouldn't meet us at all.

It was November 22, Pete's and my twenty-fifth wedding anniversary, when we made that drive to John Day. This wasn't just a quick hop across town—John Day is a three-hour drive from Bend, and round-trip would take us most of the day. But that's how we chose to spend our anniversary—with the hope of seeing our daughter and seizing the chance to snag the car.

Maggie met us at the impound yard when we arrived in town. She and I hugged like old friends. Pete handled things in the office and settled up with the towing company while Maggie and I chattered. From our previous conversations we'd discovered a shared love of God, and it always intrigues me how that common connection can bring such immediate familiarity with a virtual stranger. As we waited for Annie, Maggie and I talked intimately about our children and agreed to pray for one another.

I wasn't surprised when after thirty minutes there was still no sign of Annie. We'd confirmed she had indeed been released from the jail, but with no way to call her and no idea of where she might be staying in town, Pete and I decided to go on our way. We said our good-byes to Maggie and then headed out in our respective cars, Pete in the Expedition and me behind the wheel of the Camry.

When the car wheels began to roll, Maggie handed me an envelope through the open window. "Read this when you get home," she said.

Annie's car seemed different than the last time I was in it. Cavernous and dirty when it sat in our garage just the month before, it was now sparkling and full of light. Someone had taken great pains to detail the interior, and it smelled of lemon. I was comforted being in the space, and on that day it seemed the next best thing to being with my daughter. I changed the settings on the radio, settled in, and all the while wondered how Annie would make it back to Bend. Would she be stuck in John Day for Thanksgiving, or was there some sort of Oregon drug trail between our two towns where she could hitch herself to someone's wagon? While there was once a time I would have made those details my business, I knew none of it was any longer up to me.

It was a beautiful drive home through the Oregon outback. The famous painted hills of that region popped with fall color. The John Day River hugs the highway for a long stretch, and I made a mental note that Pete and I should fish there someday. We caravanned the entire way home and rolled into our driveway just as it was getting dark.

Our anniversary celebration that night consisted of a quick spin around the family room to music from our wedding processional, and then a wine toast in our silver goblets—a wedding gift we brought out on the same day each year. Pete surprised me with a diamond pendant he'd purchased from our friend's jewelry store, and then we crashed on the couch, exhausted from the day's activity.

I had taken the envelope Maggie gave me over to the couch and opened it as I kicked my feet up onto the coffee table. The outside of the envelope said the contents contained a prophetic word that a friend had given to her, and she was now giving it to me. Inside it read:

> "Restrain your voice from weeping
> > and your eyes from tears,
> for your work will be rewarded,"
> > > > declares the LORD.
> "They will return from the land of the enemy.
> So there is hope for your descendants,"
> > > > declares the LORD.
> "Your children will return to their own land."
> > > JEREMIAH 31:16 – 17

The Jeremiah passage was tacked to our refrigerator for the next year. It was a constant reminder that I'd put Annie into God's hands, and I believed it to be no coincidence that Maggie and I had been brought together. I trusted that God was watching over both of us—and both of our children.

Annie's car sat on the parking pad in our side yard until it was sold eight months later. She never drove it again.

CHAPTER 15

# Our Secrets Make Us Sick

I'm a talker. It's my nature to engage with waiters, banter with the cashiers at the supermarket, or talk with passersby when Pete and I walk our dog. I like to get personal, and this aspect of my personality drove my kids nuts all the years they were growing up.

"Ugh, Mom, you talk to absolutely everybody. Let's *go*."

I come from a family of mostly extroverts, but I married a man from a host of introverts, and when Pete and I produced offspring more like him, I became a stranger in my own house. For years the family joke was, "Whose job is it to talk to Mom today?" Then the three of them would all yell, "Not it!"

I've often said that I'll tell anyone virtually anything about myself. "TMI" (too much information), as Jeff has been known to say. I keep the confidences of others closely guarded but openly share about myself. I also have this thing about the truth. Unless it would hurt someone to do otherwise, I tell the truth about things. I suppose it's this propensity to talk and to share honestly about my life that helped me not get stuck in a dark secret about Annie's addiction.

It's said that addiction is a family disease, and I do know that some people suffer alone and in private about the things they don't want others to know. Recovery programs refer to this very thing with a well-known slogan that reads, "You're as sick as your secrets." Secrets can become lies, which become burdens, which become manipulations, and so on.

Cliff, a new friend from drug prevention coalition work, recently told me about the heroin addiction of his best friend from high school. The friend was apparently an exceedingly bright, popular guy, but his life unraveled through his abuse of prescription painkillers. Switching eventually to heroin, the cheaper and more readily available alternative, the friend then suffered an overdose that landed him in the emergency room.

The boy's father, a physician, happened to be at the hospital at the time. He reportedly initiated a complete cover-up of the event. Once the boy was out of danger, he and his father returned home in silence. Not even the boy's mother was told about the emergency. There was no counseling, no treatment—just secrecy and admonishment for having compromised reputations. And at what cost? Within weeks there was another overdose. This time the boy's mother found her son, completely unresponsive and near death. It's a miracle the boy survived the first overdose, let alone the second. As I understand it, he has yet to survive the secrets. He's still using drugs.

There are certainly times for discretion, both personally and professionally, but making addiction the family's dirty little secret compromises everyone's health. It can lead to sick behavior and perpetuate further addiction. Without even realizing what a healthy choice it was at the time, Pete and I began telling our friends and family about Annie's drug use as soon as it began. Talking about it gave an outlet for our despair. Rather than facing judgment, we were loved and embraced. I even spoke with some of my business clients about it, and many had their own painful stories of addiction to tell.

What I came to realize is that when I was real about my life, it seemed to give others permission to be real about their own lives.

• • •

The business suite in which Pete and I had our offices downtown was down the hall from Sally, a woman who ran a small teddy bear shop. Sally was friendly and boisterous, with a laugh to match her long red hair. She had a way of making everyone who entered her shop feel special. Because of its proximity to the women's restroom, I was in Sally's shop almost daily.

One afternoon, while I was draped over Sally's front counter as she tallied her receipts, she asked if there was any news about Annie.

"Not much. Same old stuff," I told her. I hesitated to whine too much to Sally, because she'd lost one of her sons in a motor-cycle accident a few years before. My troubles seemed to pale in comparison, but Sally saw things differently.

"I think it's worse for you than it was for me," she said. "I lost my son once, and it was absolutely terrible. But I ultimately learned how to deal with it and was able to move forward. You lose Annie over and over again. The pain is never over for you. "

Sally took me into her arms when I began to cry. She held me as a mother would have as I sobbed out all of my grief and longing. I'd never cried like that with anyone before except Pete—not even with my own mother. But I felt safe in Sally's arms as she offered me compassion.

The kindness of others, during my darkest times, could only be claimed when I was willing to throw open the shutters. Your secrets can make you sick, but your life lived authentically can help you heal.

• • •

Thanksgiving Day arrived two days after our anniversary trek to John Day. Annie had always helped me prepare the hot curried fruit dish, one of my mom's specialties, but this was the second Thanksgiving she'd be absent from the family table.

The Sunday after Thanksgiving was when I traditionally crafted the Christmas letter I've been sending out for twenty years, but this year I couldn't imagine writing my usually sappy accounting of our lives:

> Dear friends—Pete and I are busy as usual with business and volunteer work. Jeff's doing well in school and making plans for college, and Annie's taking a break from her studies to pursue her interest in meth, having moved out of her apartment and into the county jail.

I sometimes felt like both actor and observer in a play gone wrong, and was constantly trying to decipher what the director had in mind. I didn't know how the saga was going to end, but I did come to realize I'd found meaning in the remarkable care we received from others as our story played out. I decided to write about that.

November
   To our dear family and friends—Some years ago, my brother, Paul, admonished me for trying to live a Norman Rockwell life. All I could think at the time was, *And that's a bad thing?* I'm here to tell you now that Norman is MIA. The painting of our lives these days looks more like *The Scream*. Many days have brought one difficult surprise after another, and dreams for our family's future have certainly been challenged.
   The biggest surprise of this year, however, is how much joy and gratitude have flourished. God is still in his heaven, and he's walking through the fires with us. Pete is still by my side, being his cute self, and Jeff is still our adorable big goon. The outpouring of love and support from friends and family has been really quite extraordinary. The embrace we feel has been of immense comfort.
   In trying times people sometimes ask, "Where is God?" Well, we have seen God—we've seen him everywhere, especially in the kind hearts of our family and friends. So as we enter the holidays and this time of Thanksgiving, our greatest

gratitude is for you. THANK YOU for being there for us, and thank you for being the embodiment of Christ in our lives.

Thank you, Robin and Gary, for all the dinners, the favors, the gifts, and listening ears.

Thank you, Paul, for *always* being there and for truly caring.

Thank you to our dear Jeff, who keeps us laughing and gives us great hope for the future.

Thank you, Auntie Pat, for being my surrogate mother.

Thank you, Bill and Marion, for being the best friends we could ask for.

Thank you, Cheryl, for your dear friendship and sisterhood.

Thank you, Beaver and Susan, Jeanie and Mark, Gary and Susan, Rich and Charlotte, for the many years of caring friendship.

Thank you, Barb O., for being my best friend on the phone.

Thank you, Sherry and Carl, for your renewed friendship and for your dear hearts. Thank you, Nancy and Izzy, our bleacher buddies, for the great new friendship. Thank you, Pastor Scott and Kari, for leading a church that "gets it."

Thank you, Dougie, for always keeping in touch and for sharing your own life. Thank you, Sally-down-the-hall, and Carrie too, for always checking in.

Thank you, Margaret, for coming back to me.

Thank you, Jan, for all the caring lunches.

Thank you, Lacy, Jessie, and Briana, for being the exceptional young women that you are. Thank you, Ron, Annette, Nikki, and Tasha, for the path between our houses that still remains.

Thank you, Troy, for being there for Pete.

Thank you, Huib and Johan, for being part of our extended family.

Thank you, David and Tom, for being there for Paul.

Thank you, Carol, for always asking and providing hope.

Thank you, Jeanine, for introducing me to Jesus.

Thank you, Rosalie, for being my connection to Mom.

Thank you to those in recovery who have given us hope.

Thank you to all of you in our MFFSG support group at the hospital who share our struggle.

And thank you to our precious Anna, who is teaching us more about love and life than Norman ever could have.

Blessings to you this Thanksgiving and Christmas season.

Barb and Pete

# CHAPTER 16

# Pete

Annie consumed my every thought. Her face was the last one my mind eyed as I submitted to the darkness of my bedroom each night, and it was thoughts of her that first entered my consciousness when I returned to the world each morning. I spoke of her constantly, and to everyone. I all but stopped strangers on the street, announcing, "My daughter's a drug addict. Please pray for our family."

It got to the point where Pete finally had to ask me for time-outs. "I love Annie as much as you do, but can we please have just this one evening when we don't talk about her? I can't process this every minute of every day the way you do."

I know Pete appreciated the passion I had for trying to find a way to save our daughter—he was suffering too. He just didn't wear it on his sleeve like I did. But there was one day when there was no wondering what he was thinking. We were sitting in the white wicker chairs on our front porch, sipping cabernet and looking west at a darkened sky as thunderheads rumbled off in the distance. Pete stepped into his feelings.

"You know, someday we're going to get that call," he said softly, his eyes welling up. "The day is coming when Annie will be found dead in some gutter, having either overdosed or been raped and beaten. And there's not a damn thing I can do about it."

And then Pete cried. It was the second time I'd ever seen my husband sob. His heaving cries revealed raw pain, and I understood then why he usually chose not to go there. From then on, I always did my best to honor Pete's requests for a moratorium on Annie talk.

It's well documented that a child's addiction has the power to destroy marriages, and I'm grateful that Pete and I were always on the same page in our decision making. The stress was immense, but I can remember only one argument. He'd made a snide remark about my codependent tendencies. Furious that my martyrdom was not being sufficiently appreciated, I ran away from home and spent the night in a motel.

But we were back on the same page again the next day.

• • •

We'd met as young professionals while working for the same Silicon Valley company during the high-tech heydays. Pete was several years older than me and then in the process of a divorce. He was looking to make a new start. I was attracted to his classic style and great wit, and thought he was the finest man I'd ever known. While he deemed me somewhat "severe" and intense, the two of us clicked.

Dating for three years before marriage, Pete and I knew each other well before making the commitment. We eased into married life without much adjustment, and there were no major surprises. We both came from solid families and shared similar values, with a common vision of the future. We wanted the same things in life.

If there was ever a point of contention in our early years together, however, it was my relentlessness in trying to get Pete to open up and talk about his feelings.

"Quit shining that light in my face," he'd say. "I'm done talking about this."

"What do you mean you're done?" I'd say. "I'm not done. We need to talk about this until we figure it out."

"No we don't."

"Yes we *do*! You have to tell me how you're feeling."

"No I don't. I'm going to bed."

Pete's ability to disengage, with so much left unsaid, made me go absolutely ape. I'd sometimes follow him from room to room to try to keep the momentum of a conversation going. I well understood the concept of introverts and extroverts, and knowing he was an "in" and I was an "ex," I simply set my sights on changing that in him. *Be more like me*, I thought.

The old adage that opposites attract was true enough for us. Pete was the perfect type B to my A. The calm he usually exuded in any situation was a stark contrast to my reactive, get-it-done intensity. When I'd spontaneously decide to rearrange all the furniture in our house, or buy a new house altogether, Pete would good-naturedly ask if I needed any help. But he knew it was usually safest to stay out of my way. He'd prefer to sit in his favorite chair and read a mystery or historical biography, or plod through the daily crossword, filling every empty space.

Don't get me wrong. Pete has been the perfect partner in equally sharing the domestic workload. He's always washed the dishes when I cooked, and tended to the garden after I planted it. He always refused to hang Christmas lights, but during the many years and Sundays when he hunkered in front of 49ers football while I sat alone in church, my husband faithfully tackled the family's weekly accumulation of laundry. Needless to say, I learned to love church without him.

When we were faced with the unthinkable loss of our first child to addiction, it was our common vision of the future, as well as our personality differences, that seemed to keep peace in the marriage. Pete would pull me down off the ceiling when I raged with insanity, just as I would sometimes evoke emotion in him or prod him into action. I tended to lead in waging our hard-fought battles on addiction, but Pete held up the rear, and he was often first out the door, especially if there was the possibility of seeing Annie.

"Hon," he said to me late one evening, "we're going to Annie's arraignment tomorrow on that new possession charge, right?"

"I wasn't planning on it," I said. "It seems like we were just there, and I don't think I can handle any more."

"Oh, c'mon. We need to go. I want to see her, don't you?"

"Not like that I don't. And she won't even be in the court-room, will she? Won't it be that webcam thing from the jail?"

"I don't care," Pete said. "I'm going with or without you. I want to stay on top of what's going on, and I want her to know I cared enough to be there."

We were both in court the next morning.

• • •

It's proven to be a good thing that Pete's not like me. There simply wouldn't have been enough room in the house for all of that emotion. We supported each other completely and never competed to have our own way. But most importantly, we didn't blame one another. We had both given Annie everything we had to give. What more could we have asked of ourselves?

# CHAPTER 17

# Choosing Joy

Jeff had just begun his senior year of high school, and while he was actively engaged in the life of a seventeen-year-old, there was always a subtle furrow of concern above his brows. He'd poke his head out of his room whenever he heard the phone ring or sensed there had been an Annie sighting.

"Was that Annie? What's going on? Is there news?"

I continually checked in with Jeff to see how he was doing. "How's your head and your heart, Jeff? You okay? How are you feeling about what's going on with your sister?"

"I'm fine," was all he'd say. The stoic Stoefen, just like his dad.

"No, really, Jeff. How are you? You must have some feelings about this. I want you to know I'm here for you. You can talk to me about anything."

"I'm okay, Mom—really. I'm good. I have great friends. I'm having fun at school and with basketball. Don't take this the wrong way, but I frankly don't think about Annie that much."

It's true that Jeff showed all the healthy signs of being a fully engaged and normal self-absorbed teenager. Ours was the house where all the kids hung out, and our rec room filled up nearly every weekend with guys and girls playing pool and watching movies. This was just the scene I'd banked on when we'd turned our stodgy, formal living room into a gathering place for teenagers.

Occasionally it was just the guys, with a dozen of them seated around the pool table playing poker. The dark green felt provided the perfect ambiance for gaming. On one particular poker night, a friend of Jeff's came through the front door with a six-pack of apple juice slung over his shoulder. I shook my head at the irony, and absolutely delighted in it.

Since the John Day trip, Annie was now without wheels and always looking for some. She showed up in Jeff's biology class one afternoon asking to borrow his car, and Jeff handed over his keys just to get rid of her. I'd told Jeff, and other old friends of Annie's, not to loan her a car or money, either of which might be used for nefarious purposes and possibly not returned. It was also part of a plan not to enable her. But Jeff didn't want to make a scene, and he was embarrassed by the visit, especially when one of his buddies said, "Hey, Jeff, wasn't that your sister? She used to be hot—what happened to her?"

I felt I needed to protect Jeff from future intrusions, so I called the school's principal and asked that Annie not be allowed on campus again. It was a hard call to make. Annie was an alumnus of the school and everyone there knew her.

I was comforted to know that Jeff was otherwise doing well and I didn't have him to add to my worry list. But what was I going to do with myself? How could I fill the Annie-sized hole in my heart? How was I going to move forward with my life in this chronic state of uncertainty and loss?

It was right around this time that we had dinner at the home of close family friends. As usual, the conversation turned to Annie. Our friends fretted about Annie too, and her absence was a loss for all who were close to us. But people could tell I was being consumed.

"You know, Barb," my Dutch friend, Huib, began, "our son had a fairly significant learning disability when he was growing up, and it affected everything in his life. I worried about it all the time. I want to give you a little bit of advice that a friend gave me at the time: Be careful not to give the neediest of your children more time than the others. No matter what the issues, all of your kids need you."

Huib described it in such a way that I've remembered it as the "Rule of 25/25/25." Equal time for each child, and don't forget your husband. It's not rocket science, but Huib's insight made a big impression on me that evening, and it's something I needed to hear. Had I been shortchanging Jeff? Had the "good kid" been getting less attention by virtue of his goodness? I became intent on not letting that happen.

• • •

For many years, October 15 was tantamount to a national holiday in our home. It's the date when basketball season is officially launched and practices begin in high schools and colleges across the country. Some colleges go so far as to schedule their first practice when the clock strikes one minute past midnight.

Pete had been an all-league player in high school, and while he didn't make the University of Oregon's varsity team, he did play freshman ball there. His dad, Art Stoefen, Annie's Bapa Art, had played center for Stanford in the late thirties. The team won the national title that year. Art received All-American honors and was later inducted into Stanford's Hall of Fame.

I'm as proud of the Stoefen basketball legacy as if I'd been born into it myself. We figured Jeff, a virtual clone of his grandfather, would also pick up the game. By senior year he was a standout player.

Pete and I threw ourselves into basketball—and into our son. As the season unfolded, we became bleacher buddies with many of the other parents. Several of us followed the team around the state. Bend is geographically isolated, and with the Cascade Mountains on one side and the Oregon outback on the other, most away games involved several hours behind the wheel, typically in inclement weather. Basketball season in Oregon means white-knuckle driving in snowstorms, ice fogs, and whiteouts.

Each trip was a mini vacation resplendent with hotel accommodations, dinners out, and sightseeing. It was a glorious distraction, and a wonderful investment not only in our son but also in our marriage.

. . .

It had been a couple of weeks since we'd fetched Annie's car from John Day. We hadn't heard from her since—that is, until she called my cell phone while Pete and I were comfortably nestled in a darling bed-and-breakfast on one of our trips to western Oregon.

"Where are you guys?" she asked.

"Hi, Annie. We're in Silverton at one of Jeff's tournaments. You okay?"

"Yeah. I've been calling the house and just wondered where you were. When will you be back?"

"Tomorrow sometime. Do you need something?"

"Nothin' really. Just calling to check in." She lingered a moment with some small talk and then hung up.

The minute I heard the line go dead, I regretted telling Annie we were out of town. We'd locked the house up tight, so I hoped there wouldn't be a problem when we got home. The ever-present knot in my stomach tightened a notch and rolled over a few times, but I willfully shooed away my worry. We were a hundred miles from home, and there was nothing I could do about it now.

The next afternoon we arrived back in Bend. Jeff was already home, having come back to town the night before on the team bus. He met us in the driveway, speaking with the kind of winded excitement he gets when something's up.

"Mom, your car was gone when I got home last night—Annie just brought it back. How'd she get your car keys?"

"What? Is she still here?" I was incredulous.

"No, she took off when I told her you'd be home soon. Some deadbeat came and picked her up."

"I hid all our extra keys in the pocket of my fishing jacket in the mudroom closet. How in the world did she find them there? And how'd she get in?"

"Dunno. All the doors were locked when I got home."

Feeling deflated and exasperated, Pete and I dragged in our suitcases from the car and then took a look around the house. Nothing seemed amiss, except the dead bolt on the mudroom door that led out to the back deck was unlocked, and the cover to the cat door was lying on the floor.

Pete and I looked at each other in amused bewilderment. Annie had kicked in the cat-door cover and crawled through. Once she found the keys, she'd obviously exited through the adjacent back door. The scenario was too ridiculous to be true. Who crawls through a cat door? Who *can* crawl through a cat door, albeit a large one? *Insane.* Our life was insane.

There was nothing funny about Annie taking my car, though. The seats in the back had been lowered, and the few things I'd had inside were scattered about. A blanket that I kept folded and stored in the back had been opened, and it looked as if she, or someone, had slept under it. And the car stank. It reeked of cigarettes—and meth. The odor clung to the interior as if it had been sprayed on. I felt violated that my car had been tampered with, undoubtedly by the kind of people I would never choose to associate with (which now included my daughter). My personal space had made a trip through that *other* world, and it made me feel dirty by having made contact with it.

• • •

Preseason basketball was wrapping up, and as the holidays approached, my brother suggested we mix it up for Christmas that year. It had been our long-standing tradition that Pete and I host Christmas Eve dinner for friends and family, typically a sit-down dinner for about eighteen. But this would be our first Christmas without our daughter.

Even if we knew how to reach Annie, it would be impossible to have her there. Christmas, like everything else, would become all about Annie. We hadn't heard from her since she'd taken that joyride in my car. If we stayed home, I felt sure she'd show up at the house, high and on fire, and render our holiday a complete disaster. We made the decision to act rather than react, and we took our Christmas to Paul's home up in Portland. Before leaving the house, we barricaded the cat door from the inside.

My brother is an accomplished cook, and he prepared a feast that Christmas Eve. It was the first Christmas I could remember in years when others did all the work and I could simply fa-la-la-la-la. I hadn't realized how much I needed a break from being in charge.

When dinner was ready, Paul called us to the dining room, and we all gathered round. It was a beautiful table. The centerpiece was a collection of every pewter candlestick Paul owned, each with a long jewel-toned taper rising out of the top. Paul had inherited our mom's antique silver napkin ring collection, and there was one at each place, with the name of the original owner engraved on the top. I was Betty. Paul also used our parents' wedding silver with the family *C* on it.

We took our seats, and each other's hands, and I prepared to say the Christmas blessing. With the exception of the woman sitting on my right, a friend of Paul's, it was just family that night. Paul was seated at the head of the table, and when I questioned the empty seat and full place setting next to him, he lit the single white votive centered on the plate.

"This is Annie's place," he said. "It is my Christmas prayer that she is back with us next year." With that, my blessing became merely muffled sobs.

Later in the evening, my cell phone rang, as I expected it might. It was Annie, and she was crying. "Where are you guys? It's Christmas Eve, and nobody's home."

"Merry Christmas, sweetheart. We're at your Uncle Paul's. What are you doing tonight?" I knew that whatever it was, it probably wasn't very Christmassy.

"I'm sitting here in the dark on the front steps of our house all by myself. You left without me?"

"You haven't been around, Annie. We had to go ahead and make our own plans. It feels terrible not seeing you on Christmas."

"Am I really that awful that you had to leave?"

"Like I said, we had to make our own plans. I love you, Annie, and we all miss you. Would you like to talk to your dad?"

Pete was on the phone with Annie for just a couple of minutes. Hearing from her made us all sad, and it certainly put a pall on the evening. But we'd done the right thing. We had to get on with our own lives.

• • •

Jeff's league games began right after New Year's, and Pete and I continued our pursuit as team groupies. We made road trips all over Oregon, enjoying the other parents and especially each other.

We were in the bleachers of the purple gym at Hermiston High School, bickering about the atrocious officiating, when I received a call on my cell from Bank of America. A woman had apparently called, posing as me, and attempted to wire $300 from my credit card to someone named Jake. The caller was unable to answer all of the security questions, however, so the withdrawal was denied. The bank wanted to know if my card had been stolen.

Annie. She must have rummaged through our bills and found the card number when she was in the house the last time. What other numbers might she have found, and what other shoes were yet to drop?

• • •

The last game of the season would also be the end of Jeff's high school career—and it was against our crosstown rival, making it the biggest home game of the season.

The "Civil War" game always packed the gym, and tensions were high that night. Jeff drew energy from the buzz of a big crowd. When the whistle blew, he was as keyed up as a racehorse at the starting gate. A deafening roar erupted as he won the tip-off, batting the ball into the hands of a teammate for the first bucket. Jeff picked up steam from there, his confidence growing with each defensive block and rebound, and he made one sprint after another downcourt for a remarkable display of airborne layups and jump shots. It was exhilarating to watch, and with each play I pinballed between tension and frenzied release.

The good guys, unfortunately, lost the game, but Jeff ended the night with twenty-eight points. He garnered the team's MVP award for the season, as well as all-league honors. It was a great finish for him.

I'd sat in the stands that night, enveloped by the din and the crowd, cheering, screaming for my son and for the team. I was soaring. Yet while my son was lighting up the stars that night, my daughter sat in a jail cell across town. What a schizophrenic moment it was as I reflected on the duality of my life. Yet I can say without hesitation that night was one of the happiest of my life. I marveled at my circumstances as unlikely generators of such joy. How was it possible it was now splashing over me, one wave after another?

• • •

That last month of basketball coincided with Jeff's finalization of his college applications. As he struggled with his own apprehensions about leaving home, getting him to sit down and crank out a college admissions essay on "a subject of personal importance" took some coaxing. However, once the subject was decided, the rest just flowed.

> She was at my basketball game last night. She'd promised to be there, but I was all too used to her broken promises. As I stood at the free-throw line, I noticed her standing across the gym at the bottom corner of the bleachers. She looked small and fragile. She was pale and wearing a dirty, baggy sweatshirt, and her visibly unwashed hair was pulled back into a

matted bun. She tried not to be seen, but was able to catch Mom's attention, drawing her from the crowd. I guessed she was looking for cigarette money.

I was embarrassed to later learn she'd encountered one of my best friends in the girls' bathroom that night and had identified herself as my sister. I was embarrassed because my sister is a meth addict. It seems surreal to say this out loud about someone I love. She's a former honor student, model, and gifted soprano—a girl who would never take a puff of a cigarette lest she compromise her singing voice. She was the gorgeous big sister who used to drive my friends and me around, and some would sweat just being in her presence. It's appalling to me to see who she has become. It is heartbreaking.

It wasn't supposed to be this way. She is the older one, and she was supposed to be my example, showing me the way through life. She was supposed to travel the road ahead and show me where the potholes are. But as I think about it, I guess she really *has* shown me the potholes because that's where she lives. My sister has no job, no address, no phone, no car, and she lives out of the (presumably stolen) pack on her back. She has been arrested. She has been to jail. She's been to treatment. Yet rock bottom has not come. She is running the streets with nowhere to go and only the like-minded to guide her.

We used to have such fun together. I'll never forget the times we lined the stairs with sleeping bags and tobogganed down. Or our trips to the local Humane Society to pick out our newest family pet. It meant so much to me just to be part of whatever she was doing. She also liked to help me with school assignments, particularly when art was involved and my regular stick figures wouldn't cut it. She looked out for me. She cared for me. But lately she is nowhere to be found. Now we only see her in a courtroom, or during a random drop-in when she's looking to mooch food or money.

For as long as I can remember, I've heard antidrug propaganda. So much so, it seems the decision to abstain would be a given. So what happened to my sister? Was her first high just a moment of weakness? I don't have the answer, but I do know that moment altered the course of her life—and that of my family. After seeing the devastation, I know now, more than ever, it's not a path I will take.

I have left my sister unnamed in this essay because I want to protect her. I do not want her name to forever be linked to the evil of drugs, and I still have hope that one day she will seek recovery.

I really want my sister back.

# CHAPTER 18

❧ • ❧

# A Line in the Sand

Jeff came home from school early one day and encountered a small brown SUV idling in our side yard alongside Annie's deactivated Camry. A tall male in a hooded black sweatshirt stood outside the car, peering into the window of the Camry's backseat. He was trying the locks. Upon seeing Jeff, the interloper jumped into the backseat of the SUV alongside a second man. The girl behind the wheel threw it into gear and sped out of the driveway.

Finding our front door unlocked, Jeff cautiously entered the house, in spite of years of counsel instructing him otherwise. Heading directly for his bedroom, he immediately began a visual assessment of the damage. His large duffel bag with the number twenty-four on it was missing. It was his travel bag for basketball, issued by the school. Also missing were several new athletic shirts and jackets, hats, and half a dozen pair of good, brand-name athletic shoes. Jeff also discovered that three checks had been ripped out of his personal checkbook. His iPod, which had been charging next to the computer, had vanished.

Jeff dialed 911 even before his despairing phone call to Pete and me at our office. By the time we arrived home, two sheriff's deputies were already in the house, and police officers throughout our area had begun pulling over cars meeting the description of the SUV.

Jeff was beside himself. "It was Annie. I know it was. I didn't see her face, but I know it was her. I saw the back of her head, and her hair was in that ratty bun she wears. How could she and those losers just come in here and do this? I worked hard for that stuff. And my basketball bag—that belongs to the school!"

We searched the house and found more missing. Gone was the camcorder from the closet, a good watch from the dresser, and Pete's good driver—the golf club Annie and Jeff had given him one Father's Day. All of my jewelry was now under lock and key, and the few pieces I wore often and kept out on the dresser did not appear to have been disturbed. Once again, our thief knew exactly where to look, and many things that could have been taken were spared.

This was our second police report filed. With no sign of forced entry, Annie was undoubtedly in possession of a door key, presumably retrieved from the house the day she came in through the cat door. Accordingly, the next day we had all the exterior locks replaced. We also activated the security system already embedded in our home and had additional motion sensors installed. I shuddered to think what it would mean for our daughter if she ever triggered those alarms.

It was more heartache and more fury to have Annie steal from us once again, even though we realized she must have been desperate to do so. But it was more than just stuff that went missing. Gone was a sense of security in our own home. Strange men had been inside. We presumed they could find their way back. In the weeks that followed, it saddened my heart to come home from the office and find my hardworking son doing homework at the computer with a baseball bat by his side.

Robin and Gary became concerned that Annie and her compatriots might next target their house. With a gorgeous home and expensive jewelry and art, Gary prepared to defend his property by moving his revolver from the safe and into his bedside drawer.

"What are you going to do, Gary? Shoot your niece?" I asked.

"Well ... no," he said, "but I might try to scare her. I'm not going to let her and those hoodlums into my house."

"Put that thing away before somebody gets hurt," I said. I posted a mental sticky note to warn Annie to stay away from her uncle.

• • •

TV shows had begun popping up about addiction, and I saw live interventions staged on *The Oprah Winfrey Show* and *Dr. Phil*. It got me thinking again about a renewed effort at treatment for Annie. I made several phone calls around town to see if any therapists or treatment professionals knew of a local interventionist, but came away with only one lead, and a weak one at that. It may have been just as well, because we never knew where Annie was anyway. How could we possibly stage an intervention? Unless, of course, the next time she was arrested she could be held long enough at the jail for us to put together a plan.

I called the undersheriff, whose job was to manage our large county jail, and asked him about the feasibility of holding Annie for a longer period of time during her next incarceration—assuming there would be one. While no plans or promises could be made until she was actually there, I was left feeling hopeful that such a scenario might be possible. He also encouraged me to stay in touch with the DA's office and with Annie's probation officer. I did both. And I spoke with the psychiatric nurse practitioner who worked at the jail. While she couldn't share any of Annie's medical issues, she was able to listen. I asked for her help in stabilizing Annie with medication during her next lodging.

But even if we could take Annie directly from the jail to a higher level of treatment than before, could we afford it? One evening Pete and I considered the idea.

"Have we done absolutely everything we can?" I asked. "If the worst should happen, I need to know we've left no stone unturned. I don't know if we could even get her there, but would you be willing to pull out all the stops and send Annie to absolutely the best treatment facility we can afford?"

"Ya know," he answered, "I've been thinking about this too. We have to throw more at this. But how do we swing it with such lousy insurance?"

"Some of the top programs are forty or fifty thousand a month," I said, "if not more, and this time I think we need to send her out of state so she can't run off as easily. That would mean travel costs as well." I repositioned myself on the couch as I churned with the idea. "Think we could pull some cash out of our retirement accounts?"

"I'm game if you are, just so long as you realize it could be money down the drain."

I went online to search out information on interventions and treatment facilities on the West Coast and stumbled upon the name Debra Jay. She was an addiction expert I'd seen on the *Oprah* show. She and her husband had written several books, and I ordered all of them. Her latest, *No More Letting Go*, advocates against the conventional wisdom of letting go and for the value of families taking action. That was great news for me, because I was still chomping at the bit to do something. Ms. Jay cautioned that leaving an addict to hit that proverbial "bottom" should be the strategy of last resort.

"Not all bounce," she said, adding that the intervention of a loving friend or relative can actually raise the bottom to a safer place.

I sent an email to her requesting treatment information and was surprised to hear back from Debra Jay herself. Realizing that a high-priced twenty-eight-day program would burn up our resources quickly, I zeroed in on a center in California that she recommended, with fees in the midranges. We could probably afford to send Annie there for three or four months. Some sort of transitional sober living arrangement would then undoubtedly be necessary once treatment was completed.

Next I called the marketing director of that center and learned everything I could about the program. It seemed to specialize in young people and reported a good success rate with meth addicts, partly because clients were there much longer than the average thirty-day stay in other programs. I really had no idea how to evaluate a treatment facility and decided to simply trust Ms. Jay's expertise. I also prayed that God would close any doors we shouldn't walk through.

• • •

Annie showed up on our doorstep a few weeks later. Apparently missing the family, she'd come for a visit. There was also a silver ring in her possession that she wanted to return. I'd purchased it on vacation in Mexico the year before and hadn't realized it was missing. Annie had some cockamamie story about demanding it back from a girl she saw wearing it, but it was evident to us the ring had been among the items she'd taken from our house. Her show of conscience in returning it was a good sign nonetheless, so I decided it was an opportune time to talk about California.

Pete, Jeff, and I all sat down with her, and I laid it out.

"Annie, you're missing your life. We love you and want to help you. I've been doing some research and found a great drug treatment program in California. They specialize in people your age, and it's apparently a unique program with good results. You'd even be close to the beach. Please, please, Annie, will you consider this?"

"You want to send me away! No way. You hate me! Screw you."

I didn't understand how offers of help always seemed to trip her switches. Annie flew into a rage. She threw the phone that was in her hand across the room, shattering it and putting a gash in the drywall. She then stormed out the door, slamming it behind her. It was raining hard outside, and she'd have a couple of miles to walk in the dark through our wooded neighborhood before finding a store or a phone. There was a time when one of us would have chased after her. Now we simply let her go.

• • •

Annie called home a couple of weeks later, asking me for a ride. I had decided long ago not to give her rides and always said no when she made these requests. I didn't want to enable her lifestyle, nor did I want to unwittingly drive the getaway car in a drug deal. But today, Annie wanted to see her therapist. I thought it an odd request since she hadn't shown interest in self-care in a very long time. I wondered if she was being straight with me, but decided to take the chance she might be reaching out. I agreed to meet her.

As often happened when Pete and I met with Annie, we got together in a public place, typically near whatever dive she was living in. Several addicts would crash at these cheap motels, all in one room, and it was rumored that some proprietors accepted drugs as payment. Once there was a room fire in one of the motels, and the two occupants were killed. Those of us from MFFSG with kids on the street held our collective breaths until the identities were revealed. Local law enforcement was well aware that a couple of these motels housed more addicts than tourists. I never understood why the DA didn't just shut them down.

Annie was on foot when we met in the parking lot of an old-time coffee shop. With snow on the ground, I knew she hadn't walked far.

She looked awful. Annie always looked awful these days. Her skin was gray, and her hair was matted and dirty. Her eyes were cold and dark, with perfect half circles under each. From head to toe, it looked as if all the clothes she wore were men's. They just hung on her. All and all, she looked like the homeless person she was. The smell of cigarettes and sweat clung to her. There was that other smell too—the foul odor of meth seeping through her skin. Some say its distinctive odor resembles urine. I hated it with everything in me.

Annie did indeed have me drive her to see her therapist, and I parked in the adjacent parking lot and watched her enter the building. I waited for her in the car for about forty minutes. When she returned, I bought us each a hamburger and a soft drink at a nearby drive-through. I didn't consider it enabling to give my daughter a meal and, as always, felt hopeful and expectant that maybe something had changed since I last saw her.

Annie seemed irritated by her session with the therapist, however. She refused to talk about it.

We lingered in the car over our burgers, eating our meal quietly as the strangers we'd become. Losing Annie in this dreadful way, and seeing who and what she'd become, was torment. I needed it to be over. While I lived in almost constant fear that Annie would die, I sometimes dared to fear she wouldn't. Would life always be this way?

I secretly wondered if it was possible to produce a bad seed. Was Annie a bad person, that is, inherently bad? Every arrest, incarceration, and break-in, every hang-up ending with vile expletives, every contact with the monster-who-used-to-be-my-daughter reopened deep wounds. It was a hurt that kept on giving. Like my friend Sally-down-the-hall had said, death was easier.

I, of course, did not want my girl to die. I just needed the pain to be over.

I finally broke the silence. "When will you be done with all of this, Annie? When will you let us help you?"

Annie's answer was grim, emotionless. "I dunno. Probably never."

I didn't know what to think. I felt emotionless myself. My daughter was in the car seat next to me, but she couldn't have seemed more foreign or further away. While there was some familiarity, there was no longer any knowing her.

We sat in silence a while longer. A boldness swelled inside of me. I couldn't bear the distance, the grief, the insanity anymore.

"Annie," I said, "I want you to know that I love you absolutely unconditionally and I will until the day I die. But I'm not willing to have an unconditional relationship with you. I don't want to go where you're going, and I don't want the life you're living to touch me or our family.

"God willing, I have another thirty years left, and this isn't how I'm going to spend them. I'm your mother, and I can scarcely believe I'm saying this, but I'm going to survive you. You're going down, sweetie, but you're not taking me with you. And you're not taking my marriage or my son either. If our family goes from four to three, then so be it. I will miss you forever."

Annie had finished eating, and she was now leaning forward in the passenger seat with her elbows on her knees and her hands clasped in front of her. I watched for a reaction, any reaction. She was still.

"Your dad and I *love* you more than you will ever know, but we won't watch you destroy yourself. If you're ever ready to step back into your life, we will help you. Our door is always open if you want to take that step. But if you choose to remain where you are, you are on your own."

When I finished talking, Annie turned her head to look at me. Her jaw had dropped slightly, and while there was a hint of disbelief on her face, she didn't say a word.

I didn't know if my speech would bring any change in Annie— I doubted it. But I realized that *I* had changed. Helicopter Mom had just crashed and burned. I'd drawn my line in the sand. It was totally out of character and totally unpremeditated, though it had been building for a long time.

In that moment I also realized something else. It was totally freeing.

*I'd decided I was going to live.*

# PART THREE

*Normal is just another setting on the washing machine.*

UNKNOWN

# CHAPTER 19

# Taking Care

It was April again. A year had passed since that Easter when Annie first told me she was using meth. She was further away from us than ever, and we rarely heard from her anymore. With the locks on the doors now changed, the windows latched, the alarm armed, and the cat door barricaded, we no longer saw evidence of her having been in the house. There might be an occasional call when she'd pose one last plea bargain for her car, but otherwise, silence.

She did call once, however, just to let us know she was "still alive." I appreciated that call, because without a car or other ID, Annie could die and we might never know about it. I heard sadness in her voice that day. Maybe she was missing us.

Soon after that call, Annie was back in jail again. The telephone number for the county jail was now a permanent entry in my address book, listed under "A" for "Annie." She called briefly to complain about the shortage of books in the jail's library, and having already read everything there, she had moved on to the Bible. I was floored—Annie reading the Bible? After she completed all of Psalms and Proverbs, she sent us a letter:

> Dear Mom and Dad—"Camp" isn't fun anymore. I'm ready
> for it to be over … You'll be happy to know, Mom, I've been

reading my Bible. My cellie and I have a little Bible study
every night after dinner, and I wrote down a few passages that
caught my attention.

Annie cited many passages in her letter, but this familiar one
grabbed me:

> Train a child in the way he should go,
>    and when he is old he will not turn from it.
>                             PROVERBS 22:6, NIV (1984 ed.)

Was she mocking me — or offering hope?

. . .

It was easy to be consumed by our grief and the drama. Robin and
Gary always offered us respite. Pete and I had dinner at their house
as often as two to three times per week, and after my requisite cry,
we'd eat and drink and play cards. They were also avid travelers,
and with a trip to Paris in the planning stages, Robin approached
me about joining her.

"Gary doesn't really want to go. He hates big cities, and think
of the fun you and I would have. We can help each other spend
money."

I was tempted by the lure of a vacation, but afraid of what I'd
leave behind. What if something happened to Annie while I was
gone? I hated to leave Pete alone to deal with whatever problems
might arise, plus Jeff had a college visit planned and his senior
prom was approaching. I felt sure I was needed at home to hold
everything and everyone together. That had always been my job,
both real and imagined, and I was good at it. I could also imagine
far too well an emergency of epic proportions to which I'd be
unable to respond while on the other side of the world. Might I
lose my one last chance to save my daughter or, worse yet, my last
chance to say good-bye?

But for how long would I keep my life on hold? I'd already
done everything I could for Annie, and from all the books I'd

read and what I'd learned in group, everything pointed toward self-care. A Parisian vacation sure seemed to qualify.

I decided to go.

I never told Robin this, but I secretly considered canceling my trip right up until the last minute. In spite of positive self-talk, leaving town felt risky. Strange as it may seem, it took courage to board the flight that day. It didn't take long, however, until bravery gave way to pleasure. Our ten-hour flight ended in Frankfurt just at sunrise. With a quick commuter hop over dark green forests and red-roofed hamlets, we arrived in Paris.

Robin and I shared a small room in a charming boutique hotel on the Left Bank. It was an eclectic part of the city, and we were close to the Seine, Notre Dame, and more cafés than we could count. We frequented the boulangerie and wine shop directly across the street from our hotel, and gave the nearby ATM a daily workout.

It was April in Paris, and flowers decorated the entire city and countryside. One day we traveled to Giverny, home to Monet's famous garden, and took photographs of the rows and rows of tulips, thousands of them, in every size and color. I had to pinch myself while walking across the famed bridge that spanned his lily pond.

On our second night there, I called Pete just to connect and to let him know we'd arrived safely. Pete had news: Annie had been arrested again and was back in jail. One has to be the parent of a drug addict to know what great news this was. She was off the street and safe, getting three squares a day, and I wouldn't have to worry what might happen to her while I was out of town. The timing couldn't have been more perfect. I was free, carefree, to enjoy my Parisian vacation.

Robin and I spent two wonderful weeks in the City of Light. Friends of hers, whom we joined there, knew the city well and took us to favorite haunts. I came to understand why the great art masters were so great, and I was thrilled to see things I'd only read about. In addition to Monet, we saw the works of Renoir and

Manet, the Degas ballerinas, and, of course, Leonardo da Vinci's *Mona Lisa*. Rodin's sculpture, *The Kiss*, was one of the most moving things I'd ever seen.

Another woman joined our small group, the sister-in-law of our host couple. Kay and I quickly uncovered our shared faith, and she began to pray for Annie and for me. Her late husband had been a U.S. Foreign Service Officer, and with friends all over the world, she engaged many in intercessory prayer. It's hard to explain, but I could almost sense the army building in the spiritual battle that was under way.

Early the first week, Robin and I took a bus tour of the city that ended at Montmartre. Artists gather there at the highest point of the city, a hill on which sits the Basilica of Sacré Cœur. It's a magnificent spot where the panoramic view of the city is all-encompassing. I was moved by the sense of history all around me and by the reverent hush as we walked through the basilica. I lit a candle for Annie and prayed for my daughter, who was sitting in a jail cell on the other side of the world. It was the same prayer I'd been praying for nearly a year.

*Lord, please protect Annie. Please free her from this bondage, and lead her into the life you created her for.*

• • •

I learned more about Annie's arrest when Robin and I returned home. Annie had spent the night at a house that had been under surveillance for months for a high level of drug activity. The SWAT team stormed the house in the early morning hours, and Annie was awakened by the commotion, apparently opening her eyes to the heart-stopping sight of a shotgun pointed in her face. Her arrest with the owners of the house was reported throughout the day on the local TV news station and in our newspaper — the same media that had reported weekly on my son's exploits on the basketball court. My daughter, Anna Christina Stoefen, was reported as a "transient" for all the world to see.

While in Paris I had been so happy to know Annie was safe

and in jail, but when I later saw the newspaper clipping, my emotions did a free fall. I love Annie's name, and Pete and I had taken such care in giving it to her. *Transient?* My daughter had a family and a home. I knew, because I created it for her. She'd had a dream bedroom where everything matched, right down to the pink-and-blue comforter set in an impressionist floral straight from Monet's garden. The bed was framed by a headboard I'd painted on the wall behind it, in the most perfect shade of pink. Annie was my daughter. She came from warmth and love. If Anna Christina Stoefen could be called a transient, it meant this possibility existed for absolutely anyone.

Pete had heard from Annie once while I was away, but I wasn't back in the house for more than an hour when the phone rang. The caller ID read "Deschutes County Jail." I steadied myself to answer.

"Bonjour!" I said. It was Annie, of course, and upon hearing my voice she began to cry.

"Mom — I've been so miserable. It was so hard not being able to talk to you."

"Sounds like this was a rough one, huh, Annie? How you doing?"

"I thought I was going to get clean the last time. It was just so heartbreaking getting arrested again." Annie paused. "So, Mom, remember the thing you said about the treatment place in California? Is the offer still open?"

I answered cautiously. "Yes, it's still open. You want to go to treatment?"

"No, I don't want to go, but I have to. I'll die if I don't."

I'd learned not to trust most of Annie's intentions or promises. Time and again they ultimately proved false. So I tried to receive her request that day with as much stoicism as possible. My heart did quicken, though, when she told me the nurse practitioner at the jail had started her on meds again. It gave me hope that she might be serious about reaching out.

I agreed to contact the treatment center to see if they had an open bed. I also needed to call the deputy district attorney to see if the DA's office would support a request for mandated treatment rather than more jail time, or worse, state prison. Annie said she'd call her probation officer. Maybe we could collectively devise a plan to present to the judge at Annie's arraignment on Friday morning. We had less than two days.

Interesting what happens when you go away and take care of yourself.

# CHAPTER 20

# A Journey of
# a Thousand Miles

The treatment center did indeed have an open bed.

"It doesn't really matter how you get her here—just that you do," the director told me. "If she wants to drink on the plane, let her. If she wants something to relax, give her a Xanax. Just get her here. Our transportation staff will meet you at the airport and breathalyze Anna then. If she's been drinking, they'll take her to detox for the night. Since she's been in jail, I think we can otherwise assume she's clean."

I also contacted the deputy DA, the woman who'd been handling Annie's case. She agreed to support a request for treatment as long as the center was a reputable one, able to provide Annie's probation officer in Bend with regular reports and accountability. This woman was handling a high-profile case in town and couldn't be in court with us on Friday, but she said she'd send a stand-in.

Annie called me again the next day, on Thursday, and much to my surprise she was still intent on treatment. She freaked, however, when I told her the plan was to take her to treatment the very next day, directly from the jail to the airport.

"Mom, I need time. I really want to be out for a while and have a few days to get used to this idea."

I was unyielding. "This is the plan, Annie. The bed is available now, and this is what everyone's agreed to. Are you in or not?"

She acquiesced.

Annie reminded me she had no clothes. With over a year of couch surfing and fending for herself on the street, she had lost everything she'd owned. Even the few things in the backpack she'd left at the scene of her last arrest were now presumably in the possession of another addict. She told me that's how things happened on the street.

"Addicts are crazy, Mom. They'll steal your stuff and steal your drugs, and then help you look for them." Accordingly, the next thing on my to-do list was to shop.

Annie and I had been together on countless shopping trips throughout her young life. We'd shopped for school clothes, play clothes, holiday clothes, and camp clothes—and clothes for school dances, dance recitals, and vocal performances. While going to school at the local community college a couple of years before, she had worked a full year for a high-end retail clothing chain and had accumulated a gorgeous wardrobe of well-cut skirts and slacks, cashmere sweaters, silk blouses, silk underwear, and an Italian leather coat and boots. All of it was gone. All of her jewelry, CDs, and collectibles—gone. She'd also had a fully stocked apartment, and with the exception of a few things still stored in our garage, all of it was gone as well. Everything was either pawned, traded for drugs, or stolen by other addicts.

I shopped for Annie that afternoon, purchasing sustenance for my daughter's next step in life. I was determined to stick to essentials, not wanting to rob Annie of the joy or responsibility of one day rebuilding her own wardrobe. I pushed a shopping cart through a low-end multipurpose department store and bought one bra, two packages of Fruit of the Loom panties, a $28 black-and-white bathing suit, one pair of jeans, two pairs of athletic shorts, a handful of assorted T-shirts, one white knit hoodie, a pair of flip-flops, a pair of tennis shoes, and socks.

It was the most satisfying shopping trip of my life.

I also put together some basic sundries, and for sleepwear I packed two of Jeff's XL T-shirts—she would love those. All of Annie's worldly possessions now fit neatly into a small carry-on suitcase. Before I zipped the bag closed, Pete, Jeff, and I each enclosed a private note to Annie, and I added a family photo.

On Friday, May 7, we were in court. Annie was brought in through a side door, in shackles and wearing the jail's standard-issue "blues." Her hair was a wild color of burgundy, and her skin pale, but her blue eyes were warm and clear. She almost looked like my daughter, and she wasn't as stick thin as the last time I'd seen her. Nearly three weeks of food, rest, and clean time looked good on her.

The sight of Annie in the custody of a sheriff's deputy strangely reminded me of the first time she'd ever met an officer of the law. It had been at breakfast one morning at a Bob's Big Boy restaurant. Annie was four, and Pete and I were playfully teaching her how to shake hands.

"Give a firm grip and look the person directly in the eye," Pete had told her. Annie focused intently on her new task. When it was my turn, I grabbed her hand.

"Annie, then you say, 'Nice to meet you, Mrs. So and So.'"

"Mrs. So and So ... who's that?" she asked.

Both Pete and I collapsed into laughter, and even Annie got the joke.

I noticed the police officer seated near us watching our antics. He approached our booth as he made his exit. "What a nice family you have," he'd said.

Annie was now fully inside the courtroom. She gave us a sheepish smile as she shuffled slowly toward the seat next to her court-appointed attorney. I'd expected to see my daughter in shackles that morning and thought I might fall apart at the sight of her in them. She'd been in bondage for so long I guess none of it shocked me anymore. I did feel a twinge of sadness, though, and took in a long cleansing breath, exhaling loudly.

I was uncharacteristically calm that morning, at peace really.

Pete was relaxed too. I heard my own mother's voice inside me say, "Don't push the river; it flows by itself." It was a quote she loved, and it had a prominent place on her refrigerator door. I figured the river was going to do its thing that day, and it wasn't going to need any help from me.

Pete and I waited hopefully as the deputy DA and Annie's probation officer presented the plan to the judge. Attention was then directed my way.

"What can you tell me about this treatment facility, Mrs. Stoefen?" the judge asked.

"Well, yes ... um ... it's in Southern California." The judge gave me a good-natured wave of his hand to get me to stand up. "It was recommended to me by a prominent addiction expert. With your permission, we'd like to take Anna there today."

"How much is this treatment program going to cost you and Mr. Stoefen?" he asked.

"About forty thousand for three months. It will be more if she stays longer. We've pulled some money out of our retirement fund."

"Forty thousand dollars?" The judge was astonished. "Surely you're joking. What is this place, a country club?"

"No, your honor. It's not fancy at all. It just has all the services we think Anna needs to get well. We believe the depression she's battled since middle school can be addressed there as well." I held on to the long wooden railing in front of me, shifting my weight back and forth from one foot to the other. I couldn't help wondering if the judge recognized Annie from the high school honors classes she'd shared with one of his sons.

"I know that treatment isn't a panacea for Anna's problems," I continued, "but we have to try. If the worst should happen, my husband and I need to know we did everything we could for our daughter."

The judge was receptive to me and stern with Annie. "Miss Stoefen, I hope you understand the seriousness of your situation." Annie already had three felony convictions on her record, one of which was burglary I, a class A felony. It was the price, or the gift, if you will, for my mother's pearls. "I'm willing to release you to your parents for treatment, but I don't want to later hear you've caused them to waste all this money on you."

The judge made it clear to Annie she would not like the consequences if he ever again saw her in his courtroom. She would be discharged from the jail later that day and remanded to our custody for the purpose of treatment. I'm not sure what the host of new charges was from Annie's most recent arrest, but it appeared they would not be a part of her record if she completed treatment, stayed clean, and kept out of trouble. Her only sentence would be four years of probation.

The deputy DA who was handling Annie's case that day beamed his excitement. "This is so great what you're doing for your daughter. Very, very cool. I wish you all much success."

I got the feeling he didn't see addicts go to treatment very often.

Annie was escorted out of the courtroom by the same sheriff's deputy and was returned to the jail across town. Her release would take a couple of hours to process, then we'd receive a call to come get her. It was already noon, and we needed to be at the airport by no later than 3:30 p.m.

Pete and I returned home to wait for the call from jail, but it never came. I finally called there about 2:00 p.m., asking if there was any way to expedite things. This seemed a bold gesture—me telling the jail to hurry up. But Annie told us later that behind the scenes there was a sense of urgency and a spirit of cooperation among the deputies. They were rooting for her.

"Anna's going to treatment; let's get this done!"

Just as the young deputy DA had suggested that morning, this was something they didn't often see at the jail.

Finally, at 2:45 p.m., Annie walked slowly out the front door of the jail and into my outstretched arms. She seemed awkward and tentative at first, and maybe a little embarrassed. The clothes on her back were all she had with her, and she looked clumsy in men's shoes without socks.

I hugged her hard. "So, are we really doing this today?"

"We are," she said with a mix of determination and resignation. Annie jumped into the front seat and, with a kiss from her dad, we were off.

We swung by the probation department, which was adjacent to the jail, to pick up a travel document from her probation officer. Without a driver's license or a passport, both of which had been lost to life on the streets, she'd need official state identification to board the flight. It was the first time I'd seen any of Annie's mug shots, one of which was the photo used on the ID. Even the best shots from her six arrests were a far departure from how Annie used to look, when she won two teen photogenic contests growing up. In one of the mug shots she was virtually unrecognizable.

I borrowed a pair of scissors from the probation officer and freed Annie's left wrist from the jail's bright orange ID bracelet. The deputies had overlooked this task when they let Annie leave the jail, so I had the honor of wielding those shears of freedom.

We arrived in the airport terminal and reached the front of the security line quickly. The middle-aged female guard lingered over Annie's travel document that bore the Deschutes County Adult Parole and Probation logo. I held my breath.

"Have you been a bad girl?" the guard asked with a twinkle in her eye.

Relieved, Annie and I both erupted in laughter, and she responded to the guard with a wry smile. "I certainly have."

Annie and I soon boarded the plane and took our seats for the flight to Portland. There we'd catch the connection to Los Angeles. I'd cautioned Annie beforehand that our layover was brief and she'd have no opportunity for a cigarette at the airport. I knew it was possible she might dash off for a smoke anyway—or make a run for it altogether and disappear into the night on the streets of Portland. But that would be something out of my control. I just allowed the river to flow.

I did, however, trail behind Annie on every trip to the bathroom or drinking fountain.

On the flight to Los Angeles it was I who wanted the cocktail. Anesthesia for flying. And when I ordered, Annie asked for one too. I could have predicted it would be Jack and Coke, her favorite and her very first drug of choice. We each had one drink, and then Annie wrote a letter to some guy she knew in jail and promptly fell asleep. Even in jail there was "some guy."

I felt a bit guilty about the drink. It was clearly enabling behavior on my part. But considering the fact that this might be her last, I figured why not? I justified it with the demands of the day. It had been a huge day in itself, and I was still jet-lagged from Paris.

We landed in Los Angeles well after dark, and the people from the treatment center were nowhere to be found. Annie and I made several attempts to find them, walking the full length of the baggage claim area multiple times. Annie then retired to the street, sitting patiently on her suitcase and chain-smoking like a fiend. I put on a cool pretense but never let her out of my sight. I just kept sending up silent prayers.

Finally, with a quick call to the treatment center, we were connected with the driver, who'd apparently gone to the wrong terminal. All kinds of things could have gone wrong in that hour we waited, but the day's events just continued to unfold according to a plan that had long ago been taken out of my hands.

Once we were in the van, the driver breathalyzed Annie, and her blood alcohol registered zero. She confessed to having a drink on the plane, however, so our first stop would be detox. We drove for a long while through the maze of LA freeways, feeling the nearly tropical California air warm us through the open windows. Everyone was easy and relaxed; the driver and his assistant were friendly and engaging. Both were in recovery themselves and now working at the center.

When we finally reached our destination, the van pulled over to the curb of a small white house sitting on a residential corner lot. It wasn't at all the institutional setting I'd expected for detox. The four of us emptied out of the van.

At that late hour, the street was quiet and still. A woman

emerged from the far side of the darkened house, brushing by a wall of hydrangeas that cast an eerie glow of amethyst and silver in partial moonlight. Her hushed tones made it seem a clandestine transfer as she took hold of the pull handle on Annie's bag and turned to escort her inside.

It was all happening so quickly. A lifetime of irrepressible mother's love swelled inside me with such force that words became impossible. All I could do was take my daughter into my arms, and with our hearts pressed together, I silently released her again.

The woman led her away. Just before both disappeared into the darkness of an open gate, Annie turned around to me and mouthed the words, *"Thanks, Mom."*

I thought I might burst.

• • •

There's a Chinese proverb sometimes quoted in recovery: "A journey of a thousand miles begins with a single step." How fitting that our mileage from Bend to Southern California had been just that.

# CHAPTER 21

# Wherever You Go, There You Are

The van dropped me off at a hotel just blocks from the detox center. After checking in, I quickly found an all-night liquor store just around the corner. The irony of buying a bottle of wine within minutes of checking my child into rehab certainly wasn't lost on me. Although the scene of me in the liquor store might have been great fodder for a rehab comedy sketch, it's not something I would have wanted Annie's counselors to know. *Oooh, it's the mother,* I feared they might have said.

I later called Pete as I sipped from my glass, and then fell deeply asleep.

· · ·

Early the next morning I met with Liz, the marketing director of the treatment center. She gave me a tour of the facility and showed me the apartment where Annie would be living. It was a four-bedroom unit with two beds in each bedroom. The house-mother had the fourth bedroom to herself. Liz said that Annie was assigned to exactly the same bed that she herself had occupied eight years previously.

"In college I'd somehow gotten it into my head that I was a rock star," she said. "I used every drug you can think of. My parents staged an intervention and brought me here. I was literally kicking and screaming."

Liz said she'd remained clean and sober since treatment. Now she had a professional job, a husband, and a young son. I hoped her success in recovery might rub off on Annie. I took comfort in knowing my daughter would sleep in the same bed, write in her journal while peering out into the world through the same window, and post our family photo on the same bulletin board over the same dresser. Maybe there would be some magic there.

The six female residents in the apartment would share one bathroom. I wondered if the Twelve Steps had a provision for the kind of serenity *that* was going to require. There was also a kitchen where the women would prepare most of their own meals, and a great room for house meetings.

Ceiling fans buzzed quietly above white walls and light-colored carpeting, and while some attempt had been made at matching décor, furnishings were simple and functional. I'd promised the judge that we weren't sending our wayward daughter to a country club, and not really knowing what to expect, I was glad to see we hadn't. She'd be comfortable but not spoiled.

The treatment center had an open program. Clients were not under lockdown, and they rode bikes between their living quarters and meetings at the main center. Rise and shine was 5:30 a.m. and began with group meditation and breakfast in the residence quarters. The first twelve-step meeting of the day followed at 7:00. Health and fitness classes, seminars on addiction, one-on-one counseling sessions, and fun time were scheduled throughout the day.

"Addicts need to learn how to enjoy life without drugs," I was told. "Many have broken their pleasure centers and need to relearn how to have fun without substances."

Clients got around town on bicycles called beach cruisers, and we'd need to get one for Annie. That would be yet another expense in addition to the large check I had written for ninety days of treatment. There was also an additional $2,000 requested to put on the books for Annie's personal needs, medications, side trips, and any other expenses that might come up.

After the tour, Liz and I came upon a large group of clients gathered on the patio outside the meeting area. I eyed Annie off to the side by herself. She looked pale and woebegone, with that burgundy hair of hers screaming loudly in the glare of the bright Southern California sunshine.

"Hi, sweetie," I said as I approached her. "How'd it go last night?"

"Oh fine. I'm tired, though. After they searched all of my stuff I went right to bed, but they brought me here way too early this morning."

"My flight leaves in a couple of hours, so I'll be taking off soon. Is there anything I can do for you before I go? You all right?"

"I'm okay, I guess. This is kinda weird, though. See that guy over there? He's loaded. Isn't this supposed to be rehab?"

"Really? He's loaded? Well, I guess someone around here will figure that out soon enough."

"Look at him, Mom. Now, really."

"I'm sure all of this has got to be pretty weird for you, Annie. But I think you'll be well taken care of. It's up to you if this is going to work or not." I turned to look at my daughter squarely. "Annie, this is your chance. This is the best your dad and I can do for you. It's a onetime deal—we don't have the resources for any do-overs."

Annie nodded slightly, then cast her gaze off into the crowd, her eyes squinting in the sun's glare.

"I love you, Annie. I have to go now." I gave her a hug and began my exit. "I'm not sure exactly when Family Week will be scheduled, but your dad and I will be back for that."

"Okay. Bye."

Leaving Annie that morning was a bit like leaving her that freshman year of college when I had wondered, *Is she going to be okay? Is she going to do the work? Is she going to make it?* But so much had changed in the five years since then. Those early hopes and dreams for my daughter's future had all gone up in smoke, through the bowl of a glass meth pipe. Unlike our college good-bye, I shed no tears. Maybe it was because my worst fears had already been realized — or nearly the worst. Now all I wanted for my daughter was that she live.

• • •

I hit the ground running when I arrived home. With Annie on such a critical task and so far away, I'm not sure how I was able to reengage in my life. Somehow I did. The busy summer was a welcome distraction, and with Jeff leaving for college at the end of August, we were awash in plans for his launch. The prospect of the empty nest only added to my feelings of loss and uncertainty.

We didn't talk to Annie much during those first weeks of treatment but sent her loving cards and notes. I asked virtually everyone I knew to do the same. I wanted Annie to be showered in *agape* love — in God's love. People from all over the world sent her cards and letters, some of them signing names she didn't even recognize.

Close neighbors of ours even visited her at the treatment center. Carrie and her daughter, Jessie, a longtime friend of Annie's, were in SoCal on vacation soon after Annie arrived there. Carrie had coincidentally sought treatment for alcoholism at the very same center a few years before, so it comforted me immensely having her check on my daughter. She reported seeing glimpses of the old Annie.

I checked periodically with Annie's case manager to see how her evaluations were coming. It wasn't long before he suggested Annie join their special program for college continuation. The center shuttled interested clients to the nearby community college and also provided tutoring and study aids for those needing extra help. This was a powerful way Annie could begin doing "normal" things again, and Pete and I were all for it. In order to complete the ten-week class Annie registered for, she committed to an additional month of treatment, and we were all for that as well. That was another big check to write, but the proceeds from the sale of Annie's car provided the exact amount needed.

Annie did call us every now and then, and it was usually to complain.

"It's too hot here."

"I don't have any clothes."

"I can't sleep."

"I hate getting up so early."

"Twelve-step meetings are stupid."

"All these Southern California girls are so rich and superficial. I don't fit in."

"This town is all concrete. Where are the trees?"

"I miss Oregon."

For as long as I could remember, Annie always wanted to be someplace other than where she was. She wanted out of "boring" Bend, but every time we were away, she wanted to go home—even while on vacation. Once in Arizona, she quickly wanted to return to Bend, but she then left for Eugene. Then it was back to Arizona a second time, and home again. I completely understood why she'd prefer Oregon to rehab, wherever that might be, but even she was beginning to see the pattern.

"Wherever you go, there you are," she told me. "That's a good one, huh?"

"Yeah, that's a good one, all right. And so true. What else are you learning, Annie?"

"That staying away from meth isn't as hard as I thought it would be, but I really want to drink. I'm only twenty-three. How am I supposed to never again have another drink? All people my age do is drink."

And drink she did. Annie's case manager called me a month into her program to report that the housemother had smelled alcohol on her breath. Annie was breathalyzed and then sent back to detox for three days. Anyone using drugs, including the drug alcohol, was always separated from the "clean" group. Each night in detox added an extra $200 to our bill, thank you very much, and her on-the-books account was quickly evaporating.

"Relapse is a part of recovery," I was told, "but we have to separate those who are using from those who aren't. Relapse can be contagious. But don't worry—this isn't a disaster. Anna will learn from this."

I guess I wasn't surprised that Annie was testing boundaries. Before embracing a lifetime of sobriety, I imagine all alcoholics need to first test the waters to see if complete abstinence is really necessary. But I didn't like the financial consequences it had for Pete and me. We've stayed in some nice hotels that were less expensive than that little white detox house.

After the three nights, Annie returned to the apartment and rejoined her housemates. But a month later she relapsed again. Annie called me, sobbing.

"Mom, I'm so miserable. I can't do this."

"Annie, you sound funny."

"I'm drunk," she said with inebriated authority. "I hate being drunk. I feel so stupid. Every time I felt this way before, meth would take care of it."

"What do you mean 'meth would take care of it'?"

"You don't feel drunk anymore, and it takes away the hangover."

"Oh." A stimulant counteracting the effects of a depressant. It made sense. Sort of. "Where'd you get the alcohol?"

"Well . . . I stole a bottle of vodka from a liquor store. Happy?"

"Oh, Annie—where are you now? Have you called the center?"

"I'm sitting on the sidewalk in front of a tattoo parlor, just all drunk. I hate this place. These meetings are stupid. I want to come home. Please, Mom, can I just come home?"

"And then what, Annie? What happens next?"

*Silence.*

"No more rescue missions, honey. You're right where you need to be. I can't stop you from leaving treatment, but I'm not going to help you do it."

"Some friends are coming to visit me. I can get a ride home with them."

"You have friends willing to drive a thousand miles to fetch you?" I doubted anyone she'd known in the past year was even capable of such a trip. "Well, just remember that if you leave, you'll have consequences to face with the judge."

"They'll have to catch me first," she said. That contentious attitude of hers was still there. I'd been assured that, over time, her hard addict exterior would ultimately soften in recovery.

"Seems to me they already did," I countered. "You know what, Annie, why don't you just quit fighting it? You could call the center right now and have someone come pick you up. Is living on the streets of Southern California where you want to be?"

"Probably not," she said.

"Let me know what you decide." I hung up.

I learned later that day that Annie did call the center, and she went back to detox, this time for five days. While she was there, another girl's boyfriend dropped a baggie of meth over the back fence, and several of the girls in residence that night, including Annie, got high. You'd think detox would be the safest place on the planet for your drug-addicted kid, but addicts are certainly resourceful people. Sadly for one of the girls, it was her first experience with meth. I guessed it wouldn't be her last.

The center never officially informed us that Annie had relapsed on meth, as they had done before with alcohol. Possibly they didn't want it known that drugs had been smuggled into detox. They may also have been protecting Annie against the potential for another possession charge. Whatever the case, Annie was open with me about it. She was upset and ashamed about the meth, and growing increasingly alarmed that she couldn't seem to stay away from alcohol. Every time she drank, it caused her to go places she didn't want to go.

I was just grateful all of this was happening under the umbrella of her treatment program. After each relapse she was welcomed back and encouraged to move forward. Had Annie been in a conventional twenty-eight-day program, I have no doubt she would have relapsed on day twenty-nine, and there would have been no safety net to catch her.

Annie returned to the center once again, but with renewed commitment. She began to actively work the Twelve Steps and was reportedly hanging out with the group of young people who were most serious about recovery. The staff noted her change in attitude, and Annie's complaining phone calls to us stopped— although she did want a cell phone.

"Everyone here has a cell phone but me. I've already picked out the one I want," she said. I could hear that old ring of entitlement in her voice.

"Annie, there is absolutely nowhere you need to call other than home, and you can do that on the house phone." I was surprised the center even allowed cell phones. It seemed an easy bridge to the old life. "We're not getting you a cell."

There was, however, a new guy in her life, and he added Annie to his cell phone plan. The phone was pink, and the man's name was Stu. He was also from Oregon. While conventional wisdom says that those in early recovery need to avoid romantic relationships, at least for the first year, the powers that be at the center turned a blind eye to Annie and Stu. By all appearances they were good for each other and supported one another's recovery. One of Annie's case managers admitted to me that she'd met her husband when they were both in treatment together years before, so she felt it would be hypocritical to run any serious interference. Annie and Stu were counseled not to flaunt their relationship, and I knew, like all the others, it wouldn't last anyway.

Annie began forming other friendships at the center as well. She became close with one girl in particular. Annie and Amanda were virtually twins. They reportedly looked alike, talked alike, and even their names sounded alike. They both were sassy and smart, and both had the same edgy discontent about them. The girls decided to call themselves Thing 1 and Thing 2, with no apparent reference to Dr. Seuss's The Cat in the Hat. Annie, the older of the two, was designated Thing 1 and Amanda was Thing 2.

Annie was now working a serious program of recovery. She was clean. She was accountable. She was going to school. And we were all learning that recovery is a process and not an event.

# CHAPTER 22

# Inner Circle

Annie had been in treatment for nearly three months when Pete and I were finally invited for Family Week. It was late July when we flew to Southern California and checked in to the same hotel where I'd stayed when I delivered Annie to treatment.

Family Week, which actually took place over four days, kicked off with a meet and greet at one of the larger residence units. It was a beautifully appointed beach home just steps from the sand. There we met Annie's case manager, as well as several counselors. About twelve families were represented in the group, and the room buzzed with anticipation—except for one grieving mother and her sister. The mother had learned her troubled daughter had run away from treatment early that morning.

The parents' meeting lasted a couple of hours, and as it neared its conclusion, our children began to arrive in small groups and gathered on the large deck outside. When the meeting broke up, we all poured out onto the deck to be reunited. Pete and I veered in opposite directions, searching through the crowd for Annie. He found her first. Beaming over the expanse of heads, he waved me over to where they stood.

The moment I caught sight of Annie I could not contain my joy. I thought the smile might break my face. After the three-month separation I wanted to inhale her. Annie's once burgundy hair was now a sun-bleached rhubarb red—gorgeous really—and it had grown several inches into a cascading mass of waves and curls. Her stark white tank top glowed against her dark suntanned skin, and her long legs went on forever beneath a short jean skirt she'd purchased at a nearby Goodwill.

Annie seemed nervous and subdued, and we approached each other gingerly.

"You look fantastic," I said as I wrapped my arms around her. "Do you feel as good as you look?"

"I'm pretty good, thanks. I feel fat, though. Tweekers put on weight when we stop using."

Annie did look heavier than what her narrow frame normally carried, but what glorious pounds they were.

"Did Jeff come?" she asked.

"I'm sorry, sweetie. He couldn't make it. He had to work. You know, Jeff leaves for college in about three weeks. Did we tell you he was recruited to play basketball?"

"Yeah, I knew that," she said softly. "It's okay; I just thought maybe he might want to come." Annie's disappointment saddened me. I wished I could make it better for her.

"Hey," she said, "I want you to meet my friend Amanda. I told you about our Thing 1 and Thing 2 thing, right?"

I'd never seen Annie so uncomfortable as she and Thing 2 giggled nervously with each other. We parents had been cautioned that our children were excited to see us, but it was a scary time for them as well. A lot had happened to all of us, and with no drugs to hide behind or to dull her shame, Annie must have felt pretty exposed that day. Facing us was the beginning of facing up to all the wreckage she'd created. The girl who took off from treatment that morning must not have been ready to do that.

We met Thing 2's mom, Laurie, a petite professional who seemed as passionate about her daughter as I was about mine. And Thing 2's brother, a recovering meth addict himself, was also there to support his sister.

What luck. It's devastating enough to have one child doing serious drugs — what must it be like to have two? I was instantly grateful for Jeff, realizing that if both my children had become addicts, I might never have been able to find my own health amid the devastation. Having at least one "normal" child felt like reassuring evidence that I at least did something right, although I have since come to believe that I'm no more responsible for Jeff's achievements than I am for Annie's floundering.

Laurie was a single parent. From the stories she shared, I could tell she'd weathered much. Having soldiered through one child's addiction, she'd just taken out a second mortgage on her house to help the second.

The six of us sat together at a large round table, sharing the light buffet lunch that had been provided. This was the first real meal Pete and I had had with our daughter in nearly a year. Being with her seemed otherworldly. It felt like she'd been returned to us from the dead.

After some socializing and taking in the rehab banter between Annie and Amanda, we parents were once again separated from our children, with a plan to reconvene as a group at another location. We were given an assignment in preparation for the afternoon session. Each parent was to write ten things they loved or appreciated about their child, as well as ten things about themselves they felt needed improvement. Our children had the same assignment to complete.

Later, all the parents and kids gathered again in the great room at another one of the residences. There was no furniture other than white folding chairs lining all four walls, forming a large circle, as well as a smaller circle inside. There were about forty of us, plus four counselors. The inside circle had only enough chairs for one family and, one by one, each took its turn in the center to publicly share its lists with one another.

It was extraordinary being a fly on the wall to the processes of these other families. Some shared traditions and lifestyles similar to our own, and the room was thick with emotion as loved ones struggled to reunite.

"Molly, I miss you so much," a girl's teenage brother said through his sniffles. "I don't like this only-child thing, and I don't want to lose you. Even the dog misses you." The girl's mother told her, "Mol, you and your brother are my greatest gifts. Our family isn't whole without you."

The family impressed me with their heartfelt intimacy. Once their turn was over, I openly announced, "I want to be in your family!" Misunderstanding my intent, Annie chimed in with, "Hey!"

I was saddened to see some families, however, who didn't know how to talk to one another and who couldn't share their feelings. One of the dads didn't even do the assignment. He let his wife speak for both of them.

"What was our answer to that one, Mother?" he said. The man had a full head of white hair and the ruddiest complexion I've ever seen. When a counselor asked why he didn't prepare his own love list for his daughter, the clueless look on his face declared that he simply didn't do that kind of thing. Besides looking like a complete buffoon, he had no discernible connection whatsoever with his daughter. The frail girl beside him sat tentatively in her seat as if it hurt to make contact with the hard plastic. Her vacant eyes were partly shielded by pink-tinted glasses. As I studied her, I couldn't help wondering if she was going to make it.

When our turn came to be inside the circle, Pete, Annie, and I positioned our chairs so we were facing each other. Annie initially looked past us, exchanging embarrassed glances and giggles with Thing 2, so I switched places with her to remove the distraction. The people surrounding us then ultimately morphed into wallpaper faces. It was now just we three, cocooned within the safety of our own inner circle. Pete wanted to go first.

"Annie, you amaze me with how capable you are. I love how smart you are and how you can beat anyone at a game of Jeopardy. You can retain more volumes of trivia than anyone I know.

I love how you love animals. I love it when you kick my butt at cribbage. I love ..."

Pete, the card-carrying introvert who was typically uncomfortable with expressing deep emotion, was able to enthusiastically affirm our daughter as he spilled out his love for her. My eyes were fixed on Annie, and I saw tears well up as she received her father's words. Pete continued, confessing his own shortcomings, his own "character defects."

"I lack patience and can have knee-jerk reactions to things. I can be too judgmental. Sometimes I drink too much." Pete and Annie exchanged knowing glances and then embraced.

While Pete and I had completed our lists separately, we had several duplications, so when my turn came I tried to talk about things he had not already shared.

"Annie, I love how much fun you are, and I love the way I feel when I'm with you. I love to listen to your beautiful singing voice. I love how clever and creative you are. I love your Rosie Perez imitation. You are an amazing writer, and I love how you can transport me anywhere in one of your stories. You have more talents than should be allowed in any one person!"

As I continued to speak my heart, the floodgates opened. My eyes never fill with those soft, delicate tears that gracefully spill down a woman's cheeks like you see in the movies. At the first hint of emotion I'm what Oprah Winfrey calls "an ugly crier." My face contorts into a puffy, mottled mess, and with gasping snorts, I'm unable to speak in normal tones. I now attempted a couple of cleansing Lamaze breaths as I battled for the composure to speak these next words to her.

"Annie, I want you to know how much I've loved being your mother, and how proud I am to be your mother. It's been a wild ride, but I wouldn't have missed it." Annie's eyes flickered with surprise, and then her expression softened as I continued. "I know I'm not perfect, as much as I'd like to be. I can be controlling, and I certainly like things to be the way I like them." Annie was now nodding in agreement, and all three of us laughed. "But, sweetie,

I'm learning to let go of some of those things, and to let go of my need to sometimes try to control your life."

Then it was Annie's turn to speak. "Thanks for hanging in there with me, you guys. You've saved my [tail] once again. I know I've been terrible, and I'm sorry." Annie drew up her bottom lip as she fought her own tears now. "I'm just so sorry for all of it. Thanks for getting me here. Thanks for being a family I wanted to come back to."

# CHAPTER 23

# It's a Disease

Day two of Family Week began with just the parents again, and we were back in the same room, with all chairs now facing forward. We were there to hear Dr. Kevin McCauley, an addiction specialist and former Navy flight surgeon.

"There's no group of people I enjoy more than pilots, except maybe for addicts," he said. "I really love addicts."

Laughter rippled through the room, and Dr. McCauley immediately had our attention.

"If all we do is look at the addict's behavior, we are going to draw some quick conclusions about who they are as a person. It is nearly impossible not to do this, because the behavior of addicts is just so shocking! We might say that addicts are 'morally weak.' Or that they have 'an addictive personality.' We may judge their character, their friends, perhaps even their upbringing to be flawed. Sometimes addicts even describe themselves in such terms. These ideas about the nature of addiction are very powerful. If we were to look at behavior alone, these ideas make the most sense as the reasons for addiction. But what if that's *wrong*?"

Suffering the day's humidity in a shirt and tie, Dr. McCauley repeatedly paused to mop his face with a handkerchief. "The truth is there is no such thing as an addictive personality. Addiction occurs in people with strong moral values, regardless of their upbringing or social environment. While moral flaws, character defects, and family dysfunction can indeed *accompany* addiction, they cannot in fact *cause* addiction."

Dr. McCauley began a PowerPoint presentation to answer the question, "Is addiction really a disease?" He claimed that some of what he had learned and would now share with us was information with "power to change the world."

Cleverly simplifying a very complex topic, he taught that the disease model used in medicine can also be applied to addiction. It goes basically like this: An organ in the body gets a defect, and the defect produces symptoms. For example, a leg (organ) is broken (defect), which produces pain and swelling (symptoms). Once the defect is corrected, the symptoms will disappear. Similarly, the model can be applied to addiction.

"But addiction is not an easy disease," Dr. McCauley said. "It takes place in a far more complex and far less understood organ — the brain. Its cause is not straightforward. And its symptoms, well, they look more like badness than symptoms."

Experiments were conducted in the 1960s using rats, Dr. McCauley told us, when it was discovered that "rats will self-administer drugs of abuse to only one specific area of the brain — the ventral striatum, also known as the midbrain. Rats will press a lever to deliver drugs to this area over and over to the point that they ignore all their other survival drives and eventually die." He shared that "studies like these have dramatically weakened the idea that addiction begins as a moral failing or personality disorder — because none of these factors are at work in rats." Rats don't weigh moral consequences.

I learned that brain scan technology now allows observation of this phenomenon in the human brain. When drugs are administered, it is the midbrain — the part of the brain responsible for survival (and that does not weigh future consequences) — that will light up. That is where drugs take effect. Activity in the frontal cortex, on the other hand—the thinking, feeling, loving, moral, law-abiding part of the brain—will show diminished activity, a result of its inability to inhibit one's drive to use drugs. This explains how addicts can sometimes do the unthinkable—the midbrain is in control and the seat of their true self is, in effect, turned off.

Dr. McCauley taught that approximately 10 to 15 percent of the population meets the definition of addiction. Who knew? The other 85 to 90 percent can be found somewhere on the continuum between nonuser/drinker and heavy user/drinker. Technology does not yet exist that can definitively differentiate a severe abuser from a true addict, so the best indicator of addiction, as Dr. McCauley defined it, is the presence of these three things: "loss of control, the presence of craving, and persistent use of the drug/behavior despite negative consequences."

Anyone can abuse substances and make poor or uninformed choices that yield negative, even deadly, consequences. This doesn't make them addicts. However, in the face of a DUI, repeated arrests, or the threat of losing one's spouse or children, an abuser can put down the drug or the bottle and walk away. Part of what distinguishes an addict from an abuser is his or her inability to do this. The addict has become literally powerless over the drug.

I'd previously learned that family history can predispose someone for addiction, but Dr. McCauley told us that genes alone don't do the job and do not necessarily doom someone to addiction. There is apparently "good evidence that genes *combined* [emphasis added] with severe environmental stress cause addiction." He emphasized that this isn't the kind of stress we usually think of in our normal, harried lives. It's extreme stress resulting from traumas such as physical abuse, rape or molestation, extreme violence or war, mental illnesses such as anxiety and depression, ADHD, or post-traumatic stress disorder. For one with a history of such stress, "drugs wouldn't just be pleasurable ... but would be instantly recognized by the midbrain as a survival coping mechanism. Such a scenario would account for the way some addicts describe instant addiction with their first drink or use of drugs. The degree of relief they felt when they first used drugs or first drank was so great that it immediately became their main way of coping."

Upon hearing this, I was certain it had been true for Annie.

The function of dopamine is another powerful component in understanding addiction. Dopamine is a neurotransmitter, or chemical of the brain, and part of the body's natural reward system. It is key to many brain functions such as motivation, learning, memorization, and motor control. Nearly all drugs of abuse have the ability to enhance dopamine transmission, and the euphoria experienced by a person in the early stages of drug use is a result of the dopamine process. It was long held by scientists that this pleasurable effect, or the "liking" of the drug, at least in part accounted for the development of addiction. It was the hedonic reward that perpetuated the drug use. The incentive sensitization theory, however, proposed by Dr. Terry Robinson and Dr. Kent Berridge, neuroscientists at the University of Michigan, suggests that the reverse may actually be true. Many individuals describe an actual decrease in drug pleasure after prolonged use, yet they experience continued craving ("wanting").

The incentive sensitization theory poses that addictive drug use in susceptible people creates very long-lasting brain changes in dopamine-related systems, leading to intense incentive motivation for drugs, or excessive "wanting" where drugs are irrationally craved. While "liking" and "wanting" drugs are strongly linked when drug use begins, only "wanting" becomes sensitized and thus more intense as addiction develops.★

• • •

★See Mike J. F. Robinson, Terry E. Robinson, and Kent C. Berridge, "Incentive Salience and the Transition to Addiction," in *Biological Research on Addiction*, ed. Peter M. Miller (San Diego: Academic Press, 2013), 392–93.

Dr. McCauley provided this enlightening list of the specific *substances* known to raise dopamine levels:

- Alcohol and sedatives
- Opiates — heroin, as well as pain medications such as Oxycontin, Percoset, Vicodin, and others
- Cocaine
- Amphetamines (meth)
- Entactogens (Ecstasy)
- Hallucinogens (LSD)
- Dissociants (PCP)
- Cannabinoids (marijuana)
- Inhalants
- Nicotine
- Caffeine
- Steroids

And here are the known dopamine-releasing *behaviors*:

- Food
- Sex and pornography
- Relationships
- Codependency — unhealthy attachment to the needs of another
- Cults
- Performance — extreme exercise, workaholism
- Collection/ accumulation — shopaholism or hoarding
- Gambling
- Rage/violence
- Media/entertainment

It was all coming together for me now. Annie's first addiction wasn't alcohol or drugs; it was *relationships*. Boys had provided her first high. Manifesting at age sixteen as a newfound sense of power and well-being, it had showed up when she'd previously felt none.

Dr. McCauley's list also helped me to understand why addicts in recovery need to abstain from *all* drugs of abuse, including alcohol. They all poke the same part of the brain. Using any of them can create new addictions, if not ultimately lead the addict back to their first drug of choice. Some treatment centers require that addicts stop smoking cigarettes for this very reason.

For as long as I can remember, the prevailing medical opinion on addiction has been that it is indeed a disease, but as Dr.

McCauley reported, and from what I've observed in my own health care recruiting business, the majority of physicians receive virtually no training in it. For a disease purported to affect 10 to 15 percent of the population, it's an affliction largely ignored by the medical community and left to the criminal justice system to manage. "Treat 'em and street 'em" is what I've heard some emergency medicine doctors say about addicts.

Addiction is sometimes called a medical problem with a spiritual solution, and addicts who do find help most often do so through twelve-step programs such as Alcoholics Anonymous and Narcotics Anonymous, as well as Celebrate Recovery, a Christ-centered program originally launched at Saddleback Church in which addicts share "experience, strength and hope" with other addicts and learn coping skills to help manage and lower their stress. What Dr. McCauley pointed out, which I hadn't understood before, is that the "serenity" sought in twelve-step programs is what helps reduce those dangerously high stress hormones. It actually helps heal the defect in the dopamine system.

When the group broke for lunch, poor Dr. McCauley never had a chance to come up for air. We parents were all over him, like bees to a hive. He had what we wanted, what we needed, and we were all clamoring for answers. Finally, someone was making sense of this mystery of addiction for us and why it had happened to our children.

Dr. McCauley continued his presentation in the afternoon, and I posed this question: "My daughter's been to jail half a dozen times, and every time she made noise about wanting to get clean," I said. "But when released, Annie always went right back to using. Was she just jerking our chain?"

"Maybe it was because she's an addict and not a criminal," Dr. McCauley said, offering a hint of sarcasm on a subject about which he obviously felt passionate.

I was stunned. *She's not? Annie's not a criminal?* Relief swept over me as I gained understanding. It was yet another one of those aha moments when the realization hit: Annie's not a criminal—

she's an addict. She's not a bad seed—she has a disease. I remembered what the sheriff's deputy had said to me: "Your daughter didn't do this—the drug did."

Everything Dr. McCauley talked about that day, and everything I'd learned up until that time, all converged in an instant at the same intersection. While Annie was ultimately responsible for her choices, as we all are, she had not chosen addiction—it had chosen her. She was one of the 10 percent.

I was able to forgive my daughter that very moment.

I was also able to forgive my father. In fact, I look back now on my dad's alcoholism with such regret. He'd been a superstar of a young man—a letterman in four high school sports, All-State in football, a Navy frogman in World War II, and an FBI agent in the 1950s. With a gifted IQ to boot, Dad was the celebrated son of a fine Arizona family. Yet the man I knew did two things: by day he worked a respectable eight-to-five job managing government security for a large aerospace company, and at night he sat on the couch and drank. By the time I was in college, Dad had graduated to daily liquid lunches, and they ultimately cost him the promotion he'd worked toward for his entire career. He retired early and in defeat. Until throat cancer took him shortly thereafter, Dad lived his last few years on the couch, alternating between sleep and drink.

I'd been so angry with my father for falling so far, and with what I now know, I wish I'd been kinder. It never occurred to our family that my dad was sick, and I don't think it had occurred to him either. He'd become everything he detested in others, and I believe he died in shame.

Annie's addiction, and my father's as well, caused me to examine my own drinking habits. I've tried to make an honest inventory of the situation. I can't honestly say I'm one who can take it or leave it when it comes to alcohol. I wouldn't like it one bit if I was faced with the prospect of never again having another drink. I love sharing a great bottle of Chianti at an Italian bistro or sipping a Manhattan cocktail from a bar stool while on a date with my husband. Possibly that means I'm at risk.

There was a brief time when my drinking habits did look suspect. When I returned to work after the depression that had followed Jeff's birth, my sleep patterns were a mess, and I'd sometimes awaken at 4:00 a.m. Desperate for more shut-eye in order to function at work, and trying to avoid prescription drugs, I'd occasionally take a shot of bourbon, as I used to see my mother do. Bourbon, the cure for most everything in my family of origin, was apparently still detectable on my breath later in the morning, even after I brushed my teeth. My boss at the time once commented on it. Embarrassed, I never did it again.

I do think I have normal drinking habits now, and it doesn't interfere with my life. I can enjoy a glass of wine or two, or occasionally some (family) bourbon, and stop. And it's not because I'm a better person or have greater self-control than my daughter or father. It's because I'm not an alcoholic. There's nothing I did or didn't do to keep that from happening. I simply have the good fortune of being among the 90 percent.

# CHAPTER 24

# Final Run

The remainder of Family Week was spent in family counseling sessions with case managers and the first exposure to Al-Anon for some parents. In the final large group session, one of the counselors, an elderly gentleman in recovery himself from numerous addictions — alcoholism, drug addiction, and gambling addiction — gave a sobering presentation about the battle ahead for our children.

"Some of your children are very sick," he said. "They need your support for what will be a lifelong battle for them. I have eight children, and half of them are addicts of one kind or another. I lost one of them to an overdose."

Another counselor told us we needed to learn to take care of ourselves. "You can't let your happiness depend on what's happening with your children," he said. "Their success or failure in recovery is not going to be up to you, and you need to get on with your own lives. Try to keep your focus off of them and on yourselves."

I'd had enough prior exposure to Al-Anon to have a head start with this kind of thinking, but it was confounding advice nonetheless. *Keep my focus off my child? Isn't that what we parents do — focus on our children?*

• • •

The full psychiatric workup that was supposed to have been completed as soon as Annie began treatment had actually just been done. I was curious about the results and asked her case manager about it.

"So what did the psych evaluation have to say about ADHD?" I asked him. "Does Annie have attention deficit?"

"Did you ever doubt it?" he chuckled. "Yes, all our indicators show she's textbook."

"I always thought so," I said, "but could never get her schools to look at it. They always told us she was too smart to be ADD."

"That's completely bogus," he answered. "Some of the smartest people in the universe are completely unplugged. Probably more than not."

• • •

When not in meetings, Pete and I hung out with Annie. It had been years since we three had seen a movie or had a meal out together. We took turns posing for photos on the beach and cruised the boardwalk. Pete waited patiently while Annie and I ducked in and out of each and every shop, looking at swimwear. It was my mother who had kept Annie outfitted in bathing suits for most of her life, so it gave me immense pleasure to channel Mom and buy my daughter a new red bikini.

Pete and I returned home, feeling guardedly optimistic after the restorative time we'd spent with our daughter. Annie had just three weeks of treatment left, and she was already transitioning to a less structured schedule. She secured a job as a barista at a local coffee shop and maintained the weekly quota of group meetings and private counseling sessions. Together we began researching a "step down" program, a sober house, for her to enter the day she left the center. Dr. McCauley had made a huge point of this.

"The most important moment of inpatient addiction treatment" he had said, "is the first hour after discharge. Where the patient goes next often determines whether or not the gains made in treatment will be retained or lost."

A sober house is simply a safe, alcohol- and drug-free living arrangement for addicts where there is oversight and accountability. While learning to live a clean and sober life, residents find that house rules, curfews, drug testing, and encouragement to attend twelve-step meetings all help to foster continued sobriety and clean time.

Even though Annie was clean, and there were glimpses of the butterfly working toward freedom, she was still bound by the persona of the old life. Often edgy and contentious, and sometimes doing the least she could to get by, she still had that air of entitlement about her. As if to say, "The regular rules don't apply to me," Annie skipped some of her required meetings, and she wasn't contributing as much to her own support as her dad and I felt was appropriate now that she had a job.

It wasn't long after Pete and I left California when Annie called our office late one morning with devastating news.

"Mom, something terrible has happened. Last night this guy I know relapsed and died. It's totally freaking everybody out."

"He died? Oh, Annie." My thoughts raced, and so did my heart. "How'd it happen?"

"It was Dylan's twenty-first birthday," she said, "and he'd just made it to ninety days clean. We were all at his apartment for a while to celebrate, but then a bunch of us left to go do something else."

"Does anyone know how it happened?"

"I dunno. Maybe he was celebrating with drugs, or maybe he got depressed after everyone left. His roommate found him this morning."

"Was it heroin?"

"Uh-huh."

"How awful." I sucked in a deep breath. "How are you? How's Amanda?"

"I'm pretty weirded out, but Thing 2 and I are hanging tight."

Annie and her friends were reeling from the tragedy, and counselors at the center went into overdrive. Once again I heard the point about relapse being contagious, especially given that this kind of stress and fear could make addicts want to use again.

It made me want to use something too. All I could think about was Dylan's mother getting the call that all parents fear. Twenty-one years old and ninety days clean—it was a day of such promise, yet now the battle was lost. Addiction ... you are so very cruel.

Within days, Annie's case manager called us with the report that she had missed curfew the night before. Annie, Thing 2, and a couple of guys had gone AWOL for a day and a night. Nobody used, but it had been a spending spree, and Annie got "inked." She had the sign of Gemini, all in blue ink, tattooed smack-dab between her shoulder blades. It's the permanent souvenir of a mischievous lark at Venice Beach.

Her disappearance was counted as a relapse, and Annie was chastised at the center and given a final warning. She was running out of coupons for more chances. It didn't much matter to her, however, because she left treatment within the week and moved into the sober house we'd found for her just a few miles away.

• • •

Stu was now out of the picture, having completed his program and gone back to Oregon. Annie and Thing 2, still friends, were in separate sober houses, and each worked jobs in a different part of town, but they got together often. With each of them now on the arm of a new guy, it felt to me as if a storm was brewing just offshore.

Annie wanted to remain in California and continue with the support system where she'd found sobriety, but with treatment now completed, her probation officer ordered her back to Oregon. An application could be submitted to the state of California requesting a transfer of her probation from Oregon to California, but that request would have to be made from home. With only a month of independent sober living now behind her, we began to make plans to bring Annie home the following month.

Within days of our initiating these plans, our phone rang late one night. It was Janet, the owner of the sober living house in California. Annie had missed curfew and wasn't responding to Janet's calls. This was not good news. Addicts who relapse will usually go into hiding and stop responding to calls—unless the call is from a dealer. Annie had cautioned me about this. "You don't have to worry, Ma, unless I stop talking to you."

Pete and I decided to keep panic at bay and wait to see how things would unfold. Annie still had the pink cell phone, and I made numerous attempts to reach her, but none of my calls were answered. The next morning Janet called us again to report that Annie never had returned that night, and it was thought that she and Thing 2 were together, now out on a drug run. It had been about ninety days since Annie's last relapse. What was it about that number that seemed to interrupt recovery for so many?

I continued calling Annie's cell for the next two days and was almost surprised when she ultimately answered.

"Hello?"

"Annie—it's Mom. Where are you? Are you okay?"

"It doesn't matter. Don't worry about me, Mom." Annie's speech was forced and slurred. The sound of dry mouth was a dead giveaway she'd been using meth.

"You're using, aren't you? Is Amanda with you?"

"Amanda's not with me anymore. I guess she went back to her house."

"It's obvious you've been using, Annie."

"Yeah."

"What are you going to do?"

"Ya know, I—oh—I have to go. I'll call you later."

"Annie, wait!" The line went dead.

I don't know why I wasn't terrified, but something in Annie's voice was different. It wasn't like when she was using before. I guess you could say she seemed "conscious," and with all the recovery she now had in her head, I pictured her at a crossroads.

"I really have nowhere to go," Annie said when she called the next day, "but I have to be clean for seventy-two hours before I can go back to Janet's."

"Can you check into a motel?"

"I have zero money left. I think there's one place I can crash, though. Man, the girls at Janet's are gonna have a field day with this. They all hate me anyway, and now they'll think I'm a threat to their sobriety."

"Annie, not all girls hate you. You need to quit thinking like that. Have you called Janet?"

"No, but I guess I will. I don't see that I have a choice unless I want to be back at Go. I'm just so sick of all of this."

"What happened?"

"So ... Amanda and I went to the bowling alley to meet a couple of guys to play pool, and while we waited we got the bright idea to have a beer. I know, I know, but it seemed like such a good idea at the time. And then one beer became two—then five. We ended up ditching the guys and went looking for meth. It's been a hellish few days, Mom."

"Where have you been staying?"

"You don't even want to know."

Sadness flickered through me. "Thank you for calling us, Annie. You know what I'm hoping you'll decide. I love you, and I'm praying for you."

"I need sleep. I'll call you when I get back to Janet's."

*Lord, please protect Annie wherever she is. Please free her from this bondage, and lead her into the life you created her for.*

CHAPTER 25

# A Prayer Fulfilled

Annie descended the steps of the small commuter plane and ambled across the tarmac, through the revolving door, and into the Redmond/Bend terminal. With an autumn bouquet of flowers in hand, Pete and I were there to welcome her home. It had been six months since Annie and I had departed for treatment through those very doors, and she was now returning to us only three weeks clean. I didn't realize at the time how very green she still was.

Annie's flight home had been delayed five hours at LAX, and with her ride unable to return to the airport, she had faced a lonely and anxious wait for what was still an uncertain departure time. She had called me from the cell phone that Stu still had not deactivated.

"Mom, this delay is freaking me out. The bars all over the airport are calling to me. How can I sit here for hours, jumping out of my skin, when all I want is a drink?"

"What are you supposed to do in a case like this? Is there someone you can call?" I wondered if life with Annie would always be a perpetual crisis and tried to gauge the seriousness of the situation. She had come too far, in spite of the relapses, to return home from rehab drunk. That is, if she'd even make her flight at all.

"I can't get a hold of anybody, and my sponsor isn't answering," she said.

"What about Amanda? Can she talk you through this — or could she come to the airport? Or what about Janet?"

"Amanda's at work and couldn't talk, and I'm not comfortable calling Janet. I did call this guy I've been seeing, but he just doesn't get it. He's a 'normie,' you know."

"Okay then, I'll check with the airlines on this end and see what we can do. Maybe there's an earlier flight with a different carrier. Stay in touch with me, Annie. I'll stay on the phone with you all day if you need me."

"Thanks, but my cell battery won't make it all day. I already checked my bag, and the charger's in it. I'm heading back out through security to have a smoke. I'll call you later."

I hung up the phone and immediately began a mental file search of all the people I knew in LA. There weren't many I was still in touch with, and how many people can you call when your alcoholic, drug-addicted daughter is in crisis? But one name quickly came to mind. It was Craig, my old boyfriend from high school. Now working in the entertainment industry and a recovering addict himself, Craig lived not far from LAX.

Referring to Craig as an old boyfriend really doesn't do the relationship justice — he was my first love. He was an adorably tall and lanky eighteen-year-old with a mischievous twinkle in his gorgeous blue eyes, and I was crazy about him. We came together at that all-important time in life when love hormones rage through your veins as a drug might, rendering you powerless over the intoxicating draw to your beloved. Nothing in the world mattered to us more than being together — except in Craig's case, drugs also mattered. I never fully understood his fascination with getting high, nor some of the accompanying bad boy behavior. And I was not the winner in our love triangle — drugs were. We didn't even break up. Our pairing of three years simply died.

While I'd lost most contact with Craig throughout the years, he and I did cross paths a few times through mutual friends, and when he'd found recovery twenty-odd years ago, he called me one evening to make his amends. The call had surprised me, and at the time I didn't understand what he was going through, nor the beauty and importance of the gesture.

I later realized Craig had been working the Twelve Steps. He was undoubtedly on step 8, which reads, "Made a list of all persons we had harmed, and became willing to make amends to them all." And step 9, "Made direct amends to such people wherever possible, except when to do so would injure them or others." I had been touched that Craig cared enough about what we'd once shared to have made that call, but now I better understood that the call wasn't about me; it was about Craig's recovery and his need to free himself from the burden of past mistakes.

He would be the perfect person to help Annie, and the scenario at hand would need virtually no explanation.

My panicked phone call to Craig that afternoon completely upended his plans for the day, but he was gracious about the intrusion and cavalier about the appointment I caused him to miss.

"I'd be glad to help, Barb. What's your daughter's cell phone number?"

Craig was soon on the phone with Annie, talking "program" and providing the support a sponsor might, standing ready to fetch her from the airport at a moment's notice. He and his girlfriend offered Annie a safe place for the night should she need it.

Life had strangely come full circle. It was an unlikely connection between my first love and my first child. On that day they were bound together by something of which I was not a part. I was not the common denominator—recovery was.

Annie made it home without taking a drink at either the airport or on the plane. She'd made it one more day. In fact, upon her arrival at home, Annie recounted her last relapse by saying, "I never again want to be one day clean. That is hell. It's so much easier to stay clean than to get clean."

A Prayer Fulfilled

*The therapeutic value of one addict helping another*
*is without parallel.*

NARCOTICS ANONYMOUS, *WHITE BOOKLET*

• • •

Now back in Bend and away from the protective bubble of treatment, Annie began the difficult and sometimes humbling work of dealing with the wreckage she'd left behind. On her third day home, she and I met with her probation officer. Annie was drug tested, and her file was updated. There were months of back probation fines to handle, and a large court fee to begin payments on. She was anxious to return to California as soon as possible and asked her PO to initiate the application to have her probation transferred.

She learned, however, that there was an outstanding warrant for her arrest in Grant County because of a missed court appearance in John Day. That would have to be cleared before the state of California could even consider her application.

The probation officer noted the marked improvement in Annie since the last time she'd seen her, which was the day she'd left for treatment. Neither Annie nor I was sure what kind of feedback, if any, her probation officer had received from the treatment center about her relapses, and we didn't mention them. I would have done so had it served a purpose to further Annie's recovery, but at this point, new consequences for past drug use seemed counterproductive.

Surprised it wasn't handled in treatment, I also took Annie to a county clinic for HIV and hepatitis C testing. While she hadn't used needles herself, the meth life is supercharged with sexuality, and she'd been with men who did. That disturbing reality is one I kept as far from consciousness as possible, but it had to be faced. I worried that bad news might impede Annie's recovery, so when we learned she'd dodged the disease bullet, I felt like doing somersaults for miles. I was equally relieved that life on the streets had not produced a baby, as it does with many. Annie would have her hands full just taking care of herself.

Back at home, Annie, Pete, and I forged a plan for how she'd bide her time in Bend. A women's sober house seemed the best solution, yet Annie was nervous about the downtown location and the proximity to her old haunts. One of the reasons we'd sent her out of state in the first place was to put distance between her and her drug network. While still on the street, she'd visited a men's sober house on a night when everyone there was getting loaded. Although that was an anomaly, she still didn't have much confidence that a sober house in Bend would be a safe place for her. The only alternative was for her to come home. It was a scary prospect for her and for us, but with Jeff now away at college, we decided to give it a go.

I worked up a contract for Annie's signature that outlined all the rules of the house:

- no drugs or alcohol
- counseling and meds, if prescribed
- submission to random drug testing on request (I purchased a kit)
- work full-time
- rent payments of $200 per month
- regular payments toward court costs and probation fees
- household chores, including the care of her cat, Peanut
- accountability for her whereabouts at all times
- no one allowed on our property without our prior knowledge and consent

Any infraction of these rules, and Annie would be out. The intention was not to be punitive but to keep appropriate boundaries. There was no way Pete and I could ever allow an active addict to live in our home.

The other part of the bargain was that Pete and I would be

respectful, treat Annie as an adult, stay out of her face, and not tell her how to work her program. Calling ours a sober house was a bit of a misnomer, because Pete kept wine stashed in our upstairs bedroom. But he didn't drink in front of Annie, and in a gesture aimed at not only keeping her safe but honoring her as well, no alcohol was served at any family get-togethers. Probably because of over-identification, I somehow got it into my head that I couldn't drink at all, so I didn't for months. I did continue to smoke a couple of cigarettes a day, however, and was now bumming them from Annie. She'd never seen me smoke before.

As the weeks unfolded, my worries about Annie wandering off or finding trouble were dispelled. When not at work, she was a hermit in our home, putting together puzzles, reading, or watching movies with Pete and me.

Pete and I took turns shuttling her back and forth to twelve-step meetings and to the minimum-wage job she'd secured at a nearby pet kennel. Caring for animals was probably the most healing thing she could do, and the many miles she walked dogs each day were needed exercise and a great serotonin builder. Annie had answered all questions on the job application truthfully, and the owner of the kennel hired her in spite of the box checked for felony convictions.

The job provided Annie with not only a paycheck but also daily accountability. Humility was a welcome by-product too. A month after she'd gone to treatment, most of her childhood friends had graduated from college, and there was Annie, walking dogs and shoveling poop. That was where her addiction had taken her, and it certainly got her attention. She seemed to appreciate the lesson and was grateful for the job. Keeping busy and maintaining a routine were key.

About a week after she arrived home, I helped her make what had become the guest room back into a bedroom for her. Through the years the pink headboard and floral bedspread had given way to inherited family antiques and a designer duvet, but we found a way to make the room hers. I set up a bookshelf for some of

Annie's recovery materials while she unpacked a couple of boxes she'd brought back from treatment. She pulled a large stack of cards and letters out of one of the boxes—the love notes I'd asked people to send her.

"What was it like for you getting all of those cards, Annie? Did you feel the love?" I asked her.

"Truthfully, it was kinda weird getting letters from people I didn't know. It was sort of overwhelming. But I grew to appreciate it. Here, you might want to see this," she said, lifting a page out of a notebook. "It's something I wrote for my addictions class. One of our assignments was to write our life's mission statement."

I took the page from her outstretched hand and read it first to myself and then aloud. "To no longer be a prisoner of myself and my demons, and to become the woman I was always meant to be, the woman I was born to be."

I could not believe what I was reading.

*Please free Annie from this bondage, and lead her into the life you created her for.*

Tightness formed in the back of my throat and tears started to well. "Annie, this was my prayer. Sweetheart, this is what I prayed for you every day—all day every day for a year. You couldn't have possibly known."

"That's trippy, Woom. Really?"

"I always knew he was there, but this is proof that God heard me. He's been with both of us. Do you even know how cool this is? My prayer became the desire of your heart. Or maybe the desire of your heart became my prayer. Whatever the case, do you see that God's been with us all along?"

*Did she just call me Woom?*

# CHAPTER 26

# Cleaning Up

Not yet ready to turn Annie loose on the road by herself, I drove her downtown one evening to attend her first twelve-step meeting in Bend. There are meetings somewhere in Bend every night of the week, and this meeting was in the fellowship hall of an old church. I dropped her off and left to run errands, returning to the parking lot outside the church about an hour later.

Once the meeting broke, Annie lingered outside afterward, sharing a smoke with someone. It was dark so I couldn't quite make out the figure near her in the dimly lit parking lot, but I was certain it was a guy. And I was annoyed that she was making me wait for her. I'd already spent so much of my life waiting for Annie.

She came to the car minutes later. As she lit up another cigarette, she told me there was someone at the meeting she'd known on the street.

"I was surprised to see him there," she said. "Last I heard he'd gone to prison. He was one *crazy* guy, but he's clean now. His name's Tom—he wants to hang out."

I could tell she was baiting me. "Well, Annie, as the designated housemother of your sober living arrangement, the answer is no! The last thing you need is to be hanging out with someone from the old life, especially a guy. Don't even go there."

"Yeah, I know," she said. "But I only knew him for like a minute. It's too bad—he's really cute."

"You think *everybody's* really cute. You need to take care of yourself. Anyway, don't you still have something going with that guy in California?"

"Yeah, yeah. Say, I'm hungry—can we please drive through somewhere?"

• • •

It was the week before Christmas when Pete, Annie, and I made the three-hour trek back to John Day to handle her outstanding warrant. Our last trip had been over a year earlier, and we all remembered it well. Annie told us that weekend had been one of her many "bottoms."

"Rick was still in jail, so I spent Thanksgiving with a bunch of tweekers I didn't even know. I was there almost a week before I could find a ride back to Bend. It was miserable."

For the first time, Pete and I hired an attorney to help Annie with the outstanding warrant. We'd intentionally stayed out of the way and let court-appointed attorneys represent her in previous court cases, but this time she was not only clean but in recovery. That fact had without a doubt become the prevailing principle in our universe. Without proper representation Annie thought she might end up back in jail, and she wasn't sure if her new-found sobriety could handle being with all the active addicts she'd undoubtedly encounter there.

The criminal attorney we found was from Eastern Oregon. He met us late that morning outside the Grant County courthouse. We four marched up the stairs to the clerk's office together, and the attorney provided documentation showing that Annie had been in treatment and out of state when scheduled to appear in court that summer. I was surprised it was that easy, but the warrant was canceled, and a new court date was set.

We then spent time with the attorney developing Annie's

defense, which would basically say she hadn't been in the car when Rick was arrested and that the drugs found were his, not hers.

We'd have to return to John Day for court in three weeks.

• • •

Next I battled the insurance company. Considered "moderate" by industry standards at the time, the total spent for Annie's four months of residential treatment was nearly $60,000. We were not wealthy by any means, and when we received the letter from our insurance carrier indicating that our measly $2,500 benefit had been denied, I prepared an arsenal for war.

The same insurance company had also denied benefits for the less costly treatment center we'd delivered Annie to the year before in Oregon. That facility was about half the cost, and Annie had been there for only three weeks. I was too crippled with grief at the time to fight them, although I had given a benefits coordinator at the insurance company a hard time.

"You won't cover this because my daughter is addicted to an *illegal* drug? So you only cover nice addictions, like to Oxycontin? You know, Oxy is just heroin in a bottle."

"Yes, Mrs. Stoefen, we cover treatment for addictions to prescription drugs."

"Even though many people do illegal things to acquire those prescription drugs?" I asked.

No reply.

"What about alcohol? Do you cover treatment for alcohol addiction?"

"Why, yes, of course," she answered.

"My daughter is also an alcoholic."

No comment.

"Would you cover a nineteen-year-old alcoholic who did not use illegal drugs?"

"Yes, we would cover a teenage alcoholic."

"Last I checked, underage drinking was a crime in all fifty states. Is it not?"

I was livid. Some drugs, but not others. Some people, but not others.

"This has got to be illegal," I said. "This must be a violation of public policy or something. You'll be hearing from my attorney."

The last thing I could afford was another attorney, but I was like a dog with a bone, and the insurance company did hear from me again. I went after them for benefits for both of the residential programs Annie had been in. I sent copies of my four-page appeal letter to the Oregon Board of Insurance, to our U.S. congressman, and to the governor of the state of Oregon. Within days I received calls and letters of support from the board and from the congressman's office. A check from the insurance company appeared in our mailbox within weeks for the full amount owed, plus an extra couple of thousand dollars. It was a drop in the bucket compared to our out-of-pocket expenses, but it was a victory nonetheless.

While too late for our needs, the very important Mental Health Parity and Addictions Equity Act went into effect in January 2011. The Act requires group health plans, and health insurance issuers, to ensure that treatment limitations applicable to mental health or substance use disorder benefits are no more restrictive than the requirements or limitations applicable to medical/surgical benefits. Under this new federal law, 80 percent of Annie's treatment would have been covered rather than the 4 percent we had to fight for.

Too bad most addicts don't even *have* insurance.

• • •

Annie and I had long talks during those early weeks after treatment. She'd lived the life of a meth addict for nearly eighteen months, but she'd really been gone for five years. She believed the seeds of alcoholism were sown that very first time she drank, and from then on, she became a high-volume drinker.

"I've *never* had just one drink, Mom. Not even in the beginning. I never told you this, but that first time I drank, it was like, wow, this fixes everything. All of my discomfort and my bad feelings about myself just went away. By the time I got to Eugene, I was drinking an eighteen-pack of beer a day. And if not that, a fifth of Jack or vodka."

"No, no. That's not possible, Annie. You couldn't possibly drink that much."

"Oh, yes, I did. Remember all the weight I gained that year? I got so puffy I didn't even look like me. I am a raging alcoholic, Mom. *Raging*."

Annie explained to me that things kept escalating, and while high on one thing she'd boldly try another. The concept of gateway drugs sure seemed to be true in her case.

"I started smoking weed that year before I left for Eugene and became a daily user when I got to school," she told me. "Then came the cocaine. I even smoked crack once."

"Crack? You smoked *crack* when you were in Eugene?" I was surprised that Annie's life could still shock me.

"Yeah, with a U of O football player, no less. Part of the reason James wanted me to go to Phoenix with him was to get me away from all of that. We didn't do any drugs in Phoenix, but we sure got drunk every day."

"Oh, Annie. I had no idea. I am not a complete fool—how did I not know? I knew you drank too much but thought the other behavior was all bipolar stuff. Did your doctors know about all the drugs and alcohol?"

"You didn't know because I didn't want you to know. Addicts are good at that. And no, I never fessed up about any of this to doctors. I think I've tried almost every drug out there except for heroin. Even once I started using meth, heroin was a line I never crossed, at least not to my knowledge. I thought only drug addicts used heroin, and for the longest time I really didn't see myself that way. It's part of the disease."

"What do you think about the bipolar diagnosis? Think it's real?"

"I can get pretty crazy sometimes. You know how reactive I can be. But I just don't know. Guess time will tell." Annie's mood changed to one of reflection. "You know what really makes me sad? My brother became a man while I was running amok. I missed not only five years of my own life but five years of his too. I wonder if it can ever be the same between us ..."

"Why don't you let him know you want to try, Annie? It may take some time for trust to rebuild, but I do think he'd appreciate knowing this is important to you."

The next time Jeff was home from college, Annie took him out to lunch and made her amends. She told me what she'd said to him.

"Just so you know, Jeff, it was me that day in the driveway in the SUV. But it's important you know I didn't take your stuff; the guys I was with did. I was up to no good elsewhere in the house. I was trying to get them to put it all back, but then you drove up in the driveway. I'm ashamed I ever allowed this to happen."

• • •

Pete, Annie, and I returned to John Day after Christmas for her court hearing. Just minutes before we headed into the courtroom with the attorney, Annie had second thoughts about her defense.

"You know—those weren't my drugs in the car that day. But they were my drugs a million other times. I don't want you guys to have to pay for this anymore, and not to diss John Day, but I really never want to come here again. I just want this to be over. I want to plead guilty. It might mean a week or two in jail, but I can handle it now."

Annie's attorney wasn't quite sure how to interpret her change of heart—pleading guilty wasn't his thing. But I was beaming. Something was beginning to change in my daughter, and not only was she taking responsibility; she was telling the truth.

Once inside the courtroom, the DA was smug about the guilty plea, and the judge was just about to dismiss Annie with eighteen months' probation and eighty hours of community service. He then remembered another point of law. After checking a manual, he added to her sentence.

"Miss Stoefen, in the state of Oregon it also says I have to suspend your driving privileges for six months. You will then be able to pay a fine and have your license reinstated."

As only Annie could do, she begged for jail time instead of losing her driver's license. But to no avail.

While we virtually got the outcome we'd paid an attorney $10,000 for—no jail time—we left John Day with something even better. Annie shone with respectability that day, and I was so very proud of her. As the next months would show, losing her driver's license proved to be yet another unexpected blessing in keeping her safe and clean.

➤•↩

# CHAPTER 27

# My Kind of People

It was the sixth car trip I'd made with Annie in one day when I drove across town one December evening to fetch her from the twelve-step meeting. She attended meetings four to five times a week, and between that and the *two* round-trip jaunts each day to her place of employment, sometimes six days a week, it was a lot like shuttling a middle schooler again. Pete and I always shared the duty, but I really liked to make the meeting run.

I was grateful for many reasons that Annie's driver's license was on ice, and proud of her that never once did she so much as stick her toe over the line in violation of the driving suspension. While all of the time on the road was a daily imposition, I at least knew where she was and with whom. And the whole recovery thing fascinated me.

Addicts in early recovery are encouraged to attend as many twelve-step meetings as possible, sometimes even more than one a day. "Ninety in ninety" is what they say—ninety meetings in ninety days is a good kick-start for forming a solid recovery support group.

Friday night meetings in Bend were held in the community center of a large apartment complex. When I pulled into the parking lot that evening, the meeting had already broken up, and fifty or sixty people were bunched together in a cascading huddle just outside the main door and down the steps. Everyone was bundled in thick winter jackets and hoods or woolen beanies, and nearly all had a cigarette in one hand and a Styrofoam cup in the other. Stereotypical as that sounds, coffee and cigarettes are part of the recovery culture of both Alcoholics Anonymous and Narcotics Anonymous, and they also represent the last vestige of dependency an addict in recovery will hold on to. Nicotine and caffeine are both on the list of substances that can raise dopamine, and as Dr. McCauley had taught us, dopamine plays a role in addiction.

Sugar is another substance that addicts in recovery use to get a boost, and many gain weight as a result. Amphetamine addicts often gain weight when their bodies, having once been in starvation mode, grab hold of every calorie they can and then store it as fat in preparation for the next famine. Our bodies are built to do that.

Annie didn't see me when I arrived, but I couldn't miss her. She stood out like a choir girl at a biker rally. With tattooed necks and arms, multiple facial piercings, and overall tough exteriors, some of Annie's new friends in recovery were, frankly, scary looking. At first glance, some were the kind of characters many people like me cross the street to avoid.

I jumped out of the car to let her know I was there and approached the group she was mingling with. Winter coats covered most of the extensive tattooing, but many of the piercings showed. Even Annie still wore a tongue ring, a holdover from her first month of college. I really hated that thing, but if wearing a tongue ring was the worst thing she'd do that day, I considered it a good day.

Among the crowd were a lot of missing teeth, another casualty of long-term meth use. The cost of a bridge or a crown is a large expense for most of us, but especially so for someone without dental insurance and with a felony record that makes employment difficult.

As I reached the group, one of the men threw his arms around me for a bear hug. "Hi, Anna's mom! How are you tonight?"

I loved my new name. "I'm doing well, Archie. How are you?"

"I'm a grateful addict today, for sure," he said. Archie had a sweetness about him that seemed a contradiction to all of his prison "tats." He'd spent much of his adult life in prison on drug-related charges but had just celebrated one year clean.

"Say, your Anna is sure doing good here. She's a little ray of sunshine in our meetings."

*Annie a ray of sunshine?* I'd never heard her called that before. She could be great fun, but sunshine?

Narcotics Anonymous (NA) is modeled after Alcoholics Anonymous (AA) with a similar twelve-step program offering "experience, strength and hope" to people suffering from addiction. AA and the Twelve Steps have their genesis in the relationship forged between two alcoholics back in the 1930s—a stockbroker named Bill Wilson and a surgeon, Dr. Bob Smith. After years of struggle and hospitalizations, and the realization that alcoholism was a "physical allergy and mental obsession," Bill W. was delivered from his obsession to drink in what he dubbed a "hot flash"—a despairing letting-go-and-letting-God moment. Later, while on a business trip to Akron, Ohio, and feeling the urge to drink again, Bill W. made desperate calls around town looking for another drunk to talk to. He was ultimately referred to Dr. Bob, also a drunk, and together they came to the uncanny realization that something miraculous happens when one alcoholic helps another.

The term "Bill W." has become synonymous with a twelve-step secret "handshake." Asking someone if they're a friend of Bill W. is code for "Are you an alcoholic/addict?" Another addict will immediately recognize you as one of them, and most nonaddicts won't know what you're talking about, so your anonymity will be protected. Similarly, most cruise ships announce twelve-step meetings in their daily itineraries of onboard events with a designation such as "Friends of Bill W. meeting at noon on the Lido deck." For those in the know, this isn't some rich man's mega-private party, and alcohol will definitely *not* be served.

While addiction to alcohol is just as devastating and as deadly as addiction to other drugs, the culture of the two organizations can look a bit different. Annie felt more identified with NA and freer to be herself there. Whether her perception was real or imagined, as a meth addict she, frankly, felt judged by alcoholics as being inferior. Apparently not all alcoholics identify with the term *addict*.

"Addicts are my people, Mom. They're the only people who really get me."

Funny thing is, I was beginning to feel addicts were my people too.

From what Annie shared with me, and with what I could glean myself by hanging out after meetings, few of these people had grown up with the stable home life Annie had. Many, like Archie, had extensive arrest records. I met people who had lost everything and everyone—homes, marriages, children, health—all devastating consequences of their drug use. Yet what struck me about virtually all of them was a renewing of the spirit that sprang from working their program. There was gratitude. Humility. Hope. Serenity.

"I can't control what someone else might do or how they might react," I'd hear someone say. "The best I can do is to just keep my side of the street clean."

Getting clean from drugs requires looking at, and dealing with, the wrong you've done and the wreckage you've created—and changing everything. Changing not only what you do and who you do it with, but also how you think. It's a humbling process, and it's what I came to love most about the addicts I met. Gratitude and humility—the world could sure use a lot more of this.

While she didn't look exactly like the others, Annie was indeed one of them. It was a lesson in "what we look like isn't who we are," and that was as true for choir-girl Annie as it was for the ex-cons with the prison tattoos I was coming to know.

Annie finally caught sight of me among the crowd and yelled, "I'll be right with you, Woom. Is it okay if we give Tom a ride home? He lives in a sober house just a few blocks away."

Tom. Wasn't he the guy we'd decided she should steer clear of?

"Okay, I guess so." I felt charitable in the eighteen-degree weather. "Can we please get going? I want to get home."

"Sure, Ma. I just need to empty the coffeepot and gather up the literature. I'm the new secretary for this meeting."

It was Annie's nature to dawdle, so I returned to the car to wait for her and get the heater going. When she finally reappeared, she was carrying a large blue plastic storage bin and was accompanied by a slim young man not much taller than she was. He raised the back hatch for her to stow the bin and then slipped into the backseat. Annie climbed in front.

"Mom, this is Tom. Tom, this is my mom."

I turned around to shake our passenger's hand. Tom was bundled in a huge brown work coat, and he wore a dark stocking cap pulled down as far as it would go. For weeks I'd considered this Tom-whom-she-used-to-know-on-the-street the enemy, and I wasn't sure what to make of the fact that I'd just welcomed him into my car. I did know I hated the hat.

In the dim light of the car I could scarcely make out the details of his face, but noticed a well-groomed "chin strap" beard and enormous deep blue eyes that peeked out below the tiny brim of his hat. His were probably the most beautiful eyes I'd ever seen, and the whites were so big and so white. The lid of each eye dipped slightly at the outside corner, just like Annie's.

"Hi, Barb. Tom." He reached for my hand and smiled broadly, revealing glistening, perfect white teeth. *Braces*, I thought. This was someone who'd been well taken care of at home.

"So, Tom, where are we headed?" I asked.

"I live on this street, just down a few blocks. I usually walk, but it's so cold tonight. Thanks so much for the lift."

"You're welcome. So what do you do here in Bend?"

"I work in construction. A guy in the program owns a construction company, and he hired my friend Mike and me. I don't know if Anna told you, but I was in prison for a year, and it's hard to get work when you have a record. I'm just so grateful to have a paycheck."

There was that gratitude again.

When Tom spoke he revealed a confidence that wasn't evident in his appearance. It was charmingly tempered by a humility for his circumstances.

I took a right out of the parking lot and headed down the street. "With the building boom around here, I bet there's lots of work, huh, Tom?" I asked.

"Sure is. We do mostly new residential construction. I'm the framer. I'm hoping to learn more of the trade and then start my own business someday."

"Good for you," I said. "Sounds like you're doing a good job of building a new life for yourself." We chatted nonstop until reaching the driveway of the home where he lived.

"What is this place, Tom?"

"It's an Oxford House. There are thousands of them all over the country."

"Thousands, really? How many of you live here?"

"There are five of us in this house, and there are a couple of other houses here in town too. We pick our own residents and enforce our own rules. Rule number one, of course, is no drinking and no using."

"Very cool. Is your family here in town too?"

"They are. I grew up in Bend, and my parents are still here. They've been really supportive in helping me get back on my feet." Tom pushed the car door open. "From what Anna's told me, you've done the same for her."

"We've sure tried, but she's the one doing the work. I'm really proud of her."

"Well, thanks again for the ride, Barb. It was nice meeting you."

"It's been very nice meeting you too, Tom. Good night."

Tom got out of the car and, with a wave to Annie, said good night and disappeared into the side door of the house.

"Nice guy, Annie. I like how he carries himself. And you're right—he's cute."

Who knew there'd be so much under that dark cap?

• • •

Annie maintained a daily routine of work and meetings over the next months. Every one of her paychecks went toward her small rent to us and paying down many thousands of dollars in credit card debt and court fees. She was making extraordinary progress at cleaning up the financial mess and spent virtually nothing on herself. She was also beginning to work down some of the community service hours she'd been assigned by the court in John Day.

Annie still chattered on the phone every few nights with her love interest back in California, and maintained her intention of returning there as soon as her probation could be transferred. Meanwhile, Annie and Tom hung out and developed a close friendship. Like many people fresh out of prison, Tom had restitution to pay and large fines to clean up before he could drive again. Pete and I were now trading off with Tom's parents on shuttling Annie and Tom back and forth to their meetings.

Tom had been adopted at birth, and it was known that his birth mother was an addict. Nothing was known about his biological father. The loving parents who raised him, however, had created a home much like our own. In fact, we four recognized each other from some early MFFSG meetings. But when Tom's drug use had escalated and he'd gone to prison, his folks had felt dejected and pulled back. They'd been through the wringer with him, even more than we had with Annie, but we four parents now had such hope for a good outcome for both kids.

The "kids" at this time were twenty-three and twenty-eight, but they seemed much younger. It's said that emotional development is arrested when an addict begins using, so that would make Annie and Tom both about eighteen. Tom would sometimes hang out at our house and watch movies with Annie, or she'd go to his sober house and play cards with him and the guys. Too tired to drive him home late at night, I even allowed Tom to sleep over a few times, and he and Annie would camp out on our great room floor in sleeping bags, parked in front of the big-screen TV. I'd never allowed Annie to be alone in her room with a boy when she was growing up, but she was an adult now, and they were just friends anyway. What did it matter?

Annie often worked early on Sunday mornings, and if it was a night when Tom had stayed over, he'd sometimes accompany me to church. One of those mornings, Tom told me about his final arrest.

"I was on this wild run and just out of control," he said. "I had this insane idea about fleeing to Hawaii, like that was going to be the solution to everything. I needed to be stopped. I know it sounds crazy, but I was glad when they caught up with me."

Tom chuckled, shaking his head at the memory.

"I was on my knees that night in my cell, Barb, and prayed that God would just take over. I was willing to do whatever it would take to get my life back. Apparently God thought it would take prison, so that's where I went."

"What were the charges?" I asked.

"Lots of stuff. Mostly possession and property crimes, and some probation violations."

"What was prison like for you, Tom? We hear how dangerous it is and how it's more of a crime school than anything else."

"I made the decision once I got there to keep my nose clean and to hang out with the people who didn't want trouble. Yeah, there are drugs in prison. I just kept away from them. And it's not like I was in San Quentin. The prisoners in Eastern Oregon weren't stabbing each other. I'd gone to treatment before and just started working my program again."

"Oh, so you'd been to treatment. How'd the relapse happen?"

"I got cocky and tended to isolate. I thought I didn't need a program anymore. It's true what they say about our disease progressing even when we're not using. I went out sicker than ever, and my use went way up." Tom dug his hands into his front pockets and stared down at his shoes. "It was bad. I don't think I ever could have stopped on my own."

Tom looked up again. "There's something else." He paused, and then he continued. "I have a son."

"You're a father? Wow, Tom." I loved hearing that he had a son. "What's his name?"

"Isaiah." Tom beamed a huge smile and nodded his head affirmatively. "His name's Isaiah. He's four."

"A biblical name, huh? I hope you don't mind my asking you this, but was he taken away from you?"

"Not legally. But yeah, both families intervened to keep him safe. I raised him pretty much on my own until he was about two and a half, and then I relapsed. I was a mess, and his mother was a mess even before I was, so her parents took over. Isaiah lives with them down in Arizona."

"What are your plans now? Are you hoping to regain custody?"

"His grandparents are doing a wonderful job raising him—much better than I could do. For the time being, I need to focus on my recovery and becoming healthy again. But I will have a relationship with my son again. He will know me—no question about it."

Pete didn't join me in church very often, so I was glad for Tom's company. I looked forward to our time together, and while I thought taking him to church was the "Christian" thing to do, I may have benefited more than he did. Tom taught me so much about the nature of addiction and recovery, and his faith inspired my own. We had long talks about absolutely everything.

One day while alone in the house, I was puttering in the kitchen and watering plants and thinking about Tom. Why did I like him so much?

It was a rhetorical question, just the buzzing of my own mind. But God heard me and answered anyway.

"It's because he's the one you've been praying for."

There was that voice again, that voice within my own. It

hadn't even been a real prayer—*Could that really have been God I'd heard, or was it a daydream, a figment of my imagination, a fluke?*

I considered what prayer Tom might be an answer to. It's true I had prayed for a friend for Annie—for a recovery partner and for someone to come alongside and be a true friend. Tom was certainly that. But the prayer that came to mind when I heard God in my spirit that day was the prayer I'd had for Annie during the many years when she was growing up. They were prayers for the man she would someday marry.

Was God telling me that Annie would marry Tom? As an addict and ex-con, he didn't exactly fit the profile of the man I'd envisioned for her, but Annie sure hadn't lived the life I'd envisioned for her either. And what about the transfer back to California and the other guy who was waiting for her? All of those plans were in the making. Yet I realized that if I'd heard God correctly, none of that would come to fruition. I decided to just wait and watch. For once in my life, I kept my mouth shut and didn't try to influence or control events. It was a mystery, and I was intrigued to see how it would turn out.

# CHAPTER 28

# Wait for the Miracle

Valentine's Day is Annie's most dreaded holiday, if you could even call it that. As it is with many women, the day is full of expectations—and in Annie's case, no guy had ever really fulfilled them. She always became either angry or disappointed.

That year she decided to lay down all expectations and just go to work and treat February 14 like any other day. I, on the other hand, was wondering what Tom might do.

When I picked Annie up from work that night, she carried with her to the car a narrow, clear vase with three long-stemmed pink roses in it, an arrangement that had been delivered to her at the kennel. A sparkly band of pink was wrapped around the neck of the vase, and the unsigned card had only three words on it. No, not *those* three words, but these: "Just for today."

It was perfect. Brilliant. I found myself rooting for him.

"Do you think these are from Tom?" Annie asked me while fastening her seat belt.

"Of course they're from Tom. Who else would they be from? Would what's-his-name-from-California be quoting twelve-step slogans?"

It was clear to me that Tom was declaring his love, but he was treading carefully. The flowers were a beautiful acknowledgment of his friendship with Annie and of their journey together in recovery. But there was also the double entendre in the message, whether intended or not. "Just for today" was a way to play it safe and not scare her off. Tom wasn't yet asking for tomorrow.

A couple of weeks passed, and Annie took a short trip to California. She wanted to see the guy there and also reconnect with Thing 2, who was still clean after the run they'd made together several months before. It was nerve-racking to have Annie traveling with her life still hanging in such delicate balance, but it was her money and her life.

She returned home rejuvenated about the SoCal relationship but troubled that Tom had gone on an alcohol bender while she was gone. Interestingly, it had been about ninety days since Tom's release from prison. There was that fragile milestone again. Although he'd been clean and sober since going to prison eighteen months before, recovery outside of prison undoubtedly presented new challenges for him. I wondered if the relapse might have had something to do with Annie leaving town, but the explanation given was about a personal family matter. Admirably, Tom turned himself in at his sober house, and in accordance with the rules, he had to leave immediately. He then moved to the outskirts of town and into the guest room of the contractor for whom he worked.

I think my opinion mattered to him, and being a proud guy, Tom never mentioned the relapse to me. According to Annie, however, he was immediately back on program, and the two of them continued to see each other as friends. In the ensuing weeks, Annie's commitment to recovery grew, as did her love of animals and an appreciation for her job. And things at home could not have been better. There was a harmony with our daughter that Pete and I hadn't experienced in many years, if ever.

One day when we were alone in the car together, Annie reflected on how great things were. "Ya know what, Woom? I never expected it to go this smoothly when I moved back home. It's pretty amazing how well we're all getting along and how well I'm doing here."

"I know. The change in you is huge. Heck, the change in *me* is huge. I had no idea Bend had such a large recovery community—not that I'd ever thought about that before." We both laughed. "Did you know all of this was here?"

"No way. And I've made so many new friends." She hesitated. "You know that saying, 'If it ain't broke, don't fix it'? I'm wondering if I should just stay here and not go back to California."

I summoned my best poker face. "That sounds like a good question to be asking yourself, Annie. You know, I never really saw you going back to California anyway."

Within a week Annie had called it quits with the guy in California, and her relationship with Tom turned a corner.

• • •

It was fun being a witness to their blossoming love over the next months as the two families continued to shuttle Annie and Tom around town. But it was a compromise to their privacy. It reminded me of my first dates in high school when the boys didn't yet drive and either parents or a sibling would take us places. We'd stand off to the side of the porch light to steal a good-night kiss, trying to avoid detection by curious eyes peering out from the car.

I don't remember seeing Annie and Tom's first kiss, but I was witness to their first fight. Trying to invoke invisibility, I slumped in the driver's seat of the car, pressing my face against the side window.

"So what you're really saying then is I'm wrong." It was a tone I hadn't heard from Tom before.

"Don't get mad. I just disagree with your take on that tradition," Annie said. "I don't think we're violating anyone's anonymity by telling outsiders we're affiliated with any one specific recovery group."

"I totally disagree, and I know I can prove I'm right."

*Ah, the age-old battle of the sexes over who's right.*

On my shifts behind the wheel, I loved joining in the conversations that ensued after a particularly interesting meeting. Annie and Tom were careful not to violate the anonymity of anyone who had attended, but they might talk about a concept or a reading.

"So, Tom, did you hear what that one guy shared?" Annie asked. "'You can't think your way into right action; you have to act your way into right thinking.'"

"Yeah, I liked that too," Tom said.

"Ooh, I really like that," I chimed in. "I think I get it, but tell me more about what it means."

"Addicts are supposed to learn new behaviors and do the things that the fellowship tells them to do," Annie said, "at least in early recovery, that is. Our heads can be a scary neighborhood, and left to our own devices we can make all kinds of screwy decisions."

"Yeah, Barb, it's like this," Tom said. "If you repeat a behavior enough times, it will become a new habit. Thinking about it won't get you there. You have to actually do it."

"Like me and exercise, huh?"

"Yeah. Intentions aren't enough. *Doing* is what matters."

"Here's another one you'll like, Mom. Someone said something about how messed up we get when comparing our insides to other people's outsides."

"Oh, man, that is great stuff, Annie. You always did that. You always thought everybody else had it together and you were the only one who felt crummy and unsure of herself. I'd like to share that saying with every teenager on the planet."

The more I learned about the Twelve Steps and the principles of recovery, the more I became certain this stuff should be taught in school. There is untapped wisdom for the whole world in the rooms of those recovery meetings.

• • •

Annie was now accompanying Tom and me to church on her Sundays off work, and our little congregation opened their arms to the two of them. With a church culture that emphasized less doctrine and more grace, it became a place of acceptance and healing for Annie and Tom. It provided a kind of rebirth for me as well. I began to notice a shift in my own beliefs, which were becoming more inclusive and less judgmental.

At the time, Pastor Scott asked all of us to read John Burke's *No Perfect People Allowed*, which is about creating a come-as-you-are culture in the church. We welcomed all who wanted to journey with us and "do life with God." You didn't have to pretend to be something you weren't or believe something you didn't. There was freedom to doubt, which as Mr. Burke said, "is not the antithesis of faith." God was big enough to handle all of it.

With Tom's encouragement, Annie began to sing again. The worship leader created a spot for her on the team. I knew some churches were persnickety about who stood up front, so I expressed my concerns to our pastor.

"Scott, how do you really feel about Annie singing with the worship team? Her life doesn't look like what's often expected of those who stand before a congregation. Please don't feel you have to allow this because I'm on the leadership team."

"It'll be no problem. Who's to say who belongs where? If I can preach, she can sing."

Even with a weekday work schedule demanding a 6:30 a.m. wake-up, Annie now gave up her Sunday mornings in bed to sing in church. It was all very un-Annie-like, and over the course of that year, the ongoing transformation occurred right before our eyes. Annie ministered to us, just as we ministered to her. God's miracle shone before us as she regularly bellowed her favorite song, "How Great Is Our God." How great indeed!

Annie and Tom began to bring their friends from recovery to our church as well. I occasionally shuttled these people to and from their sober houses on Sunday mornings, much as I had the neighbor girls when Annie was growing up. Tom occasionally brought his roommate and coworker, Mike, and others fresh out of prison visited as well. Pete and I sometimes offered lunch at our house afterward and put everybody to work on our property, either raking pine needles or hauling brush. Food and gas money was a welcome wage for a felon who hadn't yet found a job.

Mike was a sweet guy who really stood out to me. Tall and lean, he was good-looking, with wiry, sandy blond hair and piercing blue eyes. He came to church in a red-and-blue plaid shirt and the best jeans he owned. Mike always carefully removed his hat, offering that it was the "respectable" thing to do. Our church was so laid back that nobody cared about hats, but Mike was insistent. He loved God and credited his faith for the progress made in recovering from his heroin addiction. Both of Mike's parents had died of their addictions, and I don't think he had a clue what "normal" even looked like, but he was trying.

That summer brought lots of change. Annie had her driver's license reinstated, and Pete and I sold her the old blue truck for a thousand dollars. It was the same truck she'd driven in high school and was the vehicle we'd been using since then to haul brush to the dump. Paint was peeling off the sides, and there was a broken window in the back.

"Well, it's a ride," she said. "I always loved this old truck, and it will get me wherever I need to go." Annie had finally let go of the Camry. What could have forever remained a deep chasm between her and her dad and me was now just part of the wreckage of her addiction past.

Tom's license was reinstated the next month. With both of them driving again, we four parents were relieved of some labor, but we had renewed concerns about what this freedom might mean for Annie's and Tom's continued recovery. I was diligent with my Al-Anon reading, trying to be always mindful that their recovery was their business and not mine, and its success or failure was not up to me. All I could do was support them in their journey.

• • •

Annie was now a year clean. On the night she would take her one-year coin at a meeting, I could hardly contain my excitement. Twelve-step programs award key chains or coins for being twenty-four hours clean, thirty days, sixty days, ninety days, six months, nine months, one year, and then yearly after that.

The first year is considered the biggest hurdle, and people in the program show up in droves to honor those celebrating an annual milestone. It's tradition for an addict's sponsor to bring a celebratory "birthday" cake for everyone to share, but Annie invited Pete and me to the meeting, and I was given permission to bring the cake. I ordered a large sheet cake, and my gushing to the bakery clerk was reminiscent of any mother planning the theme for a child's birthday.

"My daughter's taking her one-year recovery coin tonight. Please be sure you copy this symbol onto the cake exactly as it shows here." When I handed her a printed copy of the group's logo, the clerk recognized the symbol. I also asked her to add the words, "Wait for the Miracle."

There are so many hard days, so many so-so days, just so many days addicts want to give up, and Annie had carried that saying inside of her. "Act as if. Fake it till you make it," she was sometimes told. Even if you're not feeling it or believing it yet, behave "as if" deliverance from your addiction has already happened. "Don't give up before the miracle happens."

It was Pete's and my first visit to one of Annie's twelve-step meetings, and many of her friends in recovery had made a special effort to be there to support her. The Friday night meeting had recently moved from the community center to the sanctuary of our church, but while the surroundings were familiar, everything else about the experience was new to me.

The early part of the meeting was chaotic. People were coming and going, and even when the secretary read the Steps, side conversations continued. People began to share, but few seemed to be listening. It was like one big classroom where all the students were ADHD, including the teacher, and I later concluded that's exactly what it was. I wanted to tell them all to hush and face forward because a big announcement was coming.

Midway through the meeting the secretary began to recognize clean times, and when she asked, "Is anyone here celebrating one year?" Annie simply raised her hand and said, "I am." The group applauded attentively, but the reaction was more subdued than I expected. I wanted a brass band to storm through the room playing "The Washington Post" march or the theme from *Rocky*. This was a day for the clanging of cymbals and for fist pumps of victory in the air, but in the meeting that night, the only clanging to be heard came from dollar-sized coins. Tom presented Annie with his own one-year coin. It was wonderful.

Annie thanked the group for helping her to make it this far, and Pete and I were able to make comments as well. We both expressed pride in Annie's hard work and commitment.

"I have my daughter back," I said. "I want to thank all of you for embracing Anna and for giving her a safe place to heal."

"I'm just so proud of you, Annie," Pete said. "I love you so much." Pete cried freely, which got Annie going as well.

After Annie's turn at celebration, attention turned to a fellow taking his five-year coin. I marveled at how an addict could go that long without a drink or a drug, and I dared to dream that would one day be Annie.

• • •

A month later, Annie traveled to Ashland, Oregon, with a girlfriend from the program who was visiting her father for the weekend. She called me from a rest stop near the Crater Lake turnoff, having just fielded a call from Tom. She was barely able to speak when I answered.

"Mom. Mike's gone."

"What do you mean he's gone?"

"He's dead. Mike is *dead*. He was at his girlfriend's house last night, and she found him in the bathtub with the needle still in his arm."

"Oh my God, Annie. What happened?" I could feel the color draining from my face. I drew up a chair to sit.

"Well, he relapsed. Seems he nodded off and drowned. Poor Tom. This can't be happening with me out of town. Will you please check on him?"

"I will—of course." Worry pounded through my veins. "Are you coming back?"

"I'm not sure what we're doing yet. We're just an hour or so from Andrea's house, and getting home is so important to her. We might just push on."

"How are you doing with this, Annie? Are you all right?"

"I'll be okay as long as Tom's okay."

"How did he seem when you spoke with him?"

"He's holding on. He's not alone, and he's doing what he's supposed to be doing." Annie was silent for a moment and then added, "Ya know what, Ma? This is an ugly, unforgiving disease, and I freaking hate it. Such a wonderful life completely wasted. You have no idea how awful it is to watch someone you care about completely self-destruct."

"You're kiddin' me, right?"

"Oh yeah ... huh ..."

Had it not dawned on her before—the pain that her dad and I had lived with? Maybe she couldn't comprehend our suffering any more than we'd been able to comprehend hers.

"Mike was doing so well. What possible sense can we make of this?" I asked.

"Some of us are just sicker than others," she said. "Mike was a heroin addict, and sometimes heroin addicts die. Probably more often than not, heroin addicts die. We'd all seen him inching back to it. You know, the boundary violation thing."

"I wanted him to make it, Annie. I want so much for all of you to make it."

"There's a saying among addicts that some of us have to die so that others can live."

"What does that mean exactly?"

"It means that when one of us dies, it's a reminder to the rest of us about the seriousness of our disease. If we want to make it, we have to be vigilant."

I hung up the phone and cried for Mike, the sweet guy who had tried so hard to do what's right.

I cried for all of them.

# CHAPTER 29

# An Alcohol-Free
# Celebration

It was unusual for Tom to call rather than Annie, although he did sometimes when he needed to borrow a tool or wanted advice about business or finances. Tom and I continued to have a friendly, easygoing relationship, and I always enjoyed hearing from him.

"Hey, Tomás, what's up?" I said when I answered the phone.

The two of them were living together now. Annie and Tom had been dating for a year when she'd announced they wanted to find a place together. At age twenty-four, Annie was definitely at a point when she needed to try things out on her own again, and while living with a boyfriend would not have been my choice for her, it wasn't my choice to make. I knew she'd be safe with Tom. In my mind, the need for sustained recovery trumped most everything else. It was the better good, without which all would be lost anyway.

The day Pete and I helped load the old blue truck with Annie's things and the used furniture we were passing on to her, it was her *eleventh* move since she first left home for Arizona State. Pete contended he had no more moves left in him.

Now on the phone, I waited to hear what Tom wanted. "So, Barb, I was wondering if it would be okay if I came over? I need to talk with you and Pete about something." Tom's tone was serious.

"Well ... sure." I was trying to size up what Tom was after. "Is everything okay?"

"Um, I'd just like to talk to you."

"It's Annie, isn't it? I've sensed that she's been out of sorts lately, and I've been kind of worried about her. You're worried about her too, aren't you?"

"I'd really appreciate it if I could just please come over. I can be there in ten minutes."

"Okay, sure. Yes, come on over." I hung up the phone and yelled out for Pete.

"Pete! Tom's on his way over. Something's up with Annie." I paced through the house, trying to anticipate what was coming. "Dang it, Pete. I knew something was wrong. Do you think she's been drinking?"

Phone calls from or about Annie could still trigger a hypervigilant reaction in me. The post-traumatic stress I sometimes experienced was real. All of my systems would go on red alert as I prepared to do battle with whatever was coming. Yet in that moment, no sooner did the question to Pete leave my lips than did the density in my boggled mind clear. I felt like such a fool. The worried furrow between my eyebrows relaxed, and a broad smile appeared on my face.

Minutes later, Tom walked through the front door of our house, trying to contain a runaway smile that betrayed his surprise for us. Proudly, he pulled a tiny black box out of the front pocket of his jeans, further proof that it was indeed God who had spoken to me in my kitchen the year before.

• • •

I opened my eyes at 3:00 a.m. and was unable to close them again. It was September 13 — Annie's wedding day!

As much as I'd tried to plan for every contingency for the wedding, I was now awake and obsessing over every detail, including last night's hiccup with the rehearsal dinner. Tom's mother had spent the early part of the week in the hospital with a fluttering heart, so there was that concern, as well as the stress of those dinner details that had fallen back on me.

Annie and I met at the hair salon early that morning. We both pounded down the caffeine to jump-start the big day. Linda had been our hairdresser for nearly twenty years, and we'd been calling her "Yinda" for nearly as long because of Jeff's onetime inability to pronounce L's. The name stuck, and Yinda seemed to enjoy having that special designation in our lives.

If Annie had any wedding jitters that morning, they certainly didn't show. She was the poster girl for serenity as she and Yinda fiddled with her hair, finally deciding on the perfect updo her veil would slip into. Annie was tickled with the results, and once she was out of the chair, I was in it.

Back at home, Annie and I stood side by side in front of the large mirror in the master bathroom as we each applied our own makeup. It was impossible for me not to reminisce about my own wedding and how my mom had stationed Pete in the doorway of her master bath as I'd applied my prenuptial mascara twenty-eight years before. She'd plopped him in a chair and handed him a bourbon on the rocks so he wouldn't think about wandering off. Like I said before, in my family, bourbon had been the cure for most everything.

"That was so Nan," Annie said. "I sure wish she could be here today."

With Annie's help, I dressed in formal black palazzo pants and a tunic-length silk jacket. It was the most expensive garment I've ever worn, including my own wedding dress. I'd considered wearing Mom's pearls, which were now back in my possession. They would have provided the perfect finishing touch, but our history with them was still too fresh. I wanted Annie's day to be unencumbered by any baggage, so I opted for large silver hoop earrings and no necklace at all.

Pete and Jeff had gotten dressed downstairs and were handsome in black tuxes, ties, and vests. Pete's silver hair shone against his black attire, in spite of the baseball cap he slapped on before heading out the door. I then caught Jeff taking one last look in the mirror, channeling James Bond as he made debonair faces. Jeff's a sucker when it comes to dressing up, and while an unlikely candidate for bridesmaid duty, he would indeed be on the bride's side of the aisle that day, just as my brother had been at my own wedding.

The rest of the wedding party arrived at the church shortly after we did. As I imagine all parents of the bride and groom do, I felt a moment's relief when my daughter's intended arrived—and on time. Tom and his groomsmen took command of the church and waited to greet our guests as they arrived. The ladies were headquartered upstairs and remained out of sight until the ceremony.

I loved the simplicity of our church building for Sunday services. While it wasn't exactly the catacombs, it reminded me of Christianity's simple beginnings, and I'd rather we spend our tithe money in the community than on the building. But the stark white walls of the old warehouse, with the ratty blue indoor-outdoor carpet and blue plastic chairs, seemed an inelegant setting for a wedding. I'd envisioned a magnificent wrought iron arch framed by snowcapped mountains or a pasture of wildflowers, but Tom wanted to be married in the church that had lifted him and Annie up during their early days of recovery. I came to appreciate his heart in the matter, and we made the church as beautiful as a warehouse would allow.

Upstairs, a foosball table was kept for the youth group, and immediately upon eyeing it, Annie quickly challenged her bridesmaids and flower girls to a raucous game. What a sight—Annie in a red tank top and two gorgeous women in short black cocktail dresses and high heels taking on two ten-year-old girls in a preteen version of the same black attire. All whooped and hollered at foosball. It was almost as if they'd forgotten why we were there. I finally had to intervene.

"Annie, you need to get dressed. You're getting married in twenty minutes!"

The photographer had arrived by this time. She snapped discreet photos of Annie as she slipped into her exquisite ivory-colored silk dupioni gown. A simple ivory veil attached under Annie's coiffed bun and fell down the middle of her back to her hips. The veil had been part of a strategic plan to conceal the tattoo on Annie's back, lest it be the bull's-eye that drew everyone's gaze during the ceremony. It did the job perfectly. Annie's only jewelry was drop pearl earrings adorned with tiny diamonds, and a lovely freshwater pearl bracelet that Tom's mom had made for her. On her feet she wore ivory-colored taffeta flip-flops.

Just minutes before three o'clock, the entire wedding party gathered behind the double doors leading into the sanctuary. In hushed voices we shared last-minute instructions and waited for the cue to begin. I eyed Tom. He gave me a nervous but determined glance. I then turned around and found Pete waiting for Annie at the foot of the stairs. He blew me a kiss and gave a confident thumbs-up. I faced forward again and steadied myself. I didn't want to have an ugly cry. Not today.

The double doors on the side of the sanctuary were opened, and the crowd's glances turned with anticipation. Music for the processional spilled from the surround system in the sanctuary. It was Michael Bublé's song, "Everything."

> You're a falling star. You're the getaway car.
> You're the line in the sand when I go too far.

Tom and his best man headed down the aisle with Pastor Scott. When they reached the front of the sanctuary, Tom's parents followed and took their seats.

With the next verse of the song, it was Jeff's and my turn. He took my arm, straightened his stance, and escorted me down the aisle to my seat. The tears I'd dreaded didn't materialize, and I was able to enjoy the moment, taking in the delighted faces of our friends. As Jeff left my side, he moved to the front of the church, taking his position on the left as an attendant of the bride.

Briana, Annie's maid of honor, and, Jessie, her one bridesmaid, followed, each on the arm of a groomsman. We were all thinking about Mike, who would have been part of the processional as well.

There was a brief instrumental when Tom's two nieces tossed ivory rose petals onto the blue-carpeted aisle as they made their way forward. Then the chorus began again, with crescendo. My beautiful girl made her entrance with Pete.

*And in this crazy life, and through these crazy times,*
*It's you, it's you . . .*

Everyone rose to honor this most glorious bride as she made her appearance. Annie began to cry with her first step into the sanctuary. She was the girl who had once been in shackles, invisible, the slave to drugs and alcohol, and it felt to me as if the gates of heaven had burst open to welcome this vision in white. As Annie moved forward, her emotion escalated, as did that of all of us witnessing that moment's miracle. She stopped every few steps to greet strategically placed friends along the inside aisle and receive long-stemmed blooms for her white calla lily bouquet. Thing 2 was among them, a new woman herself, and one who still shared the exact same clean date as Annie's.

Who would have thought it possible? From despair to celebration. From being lost to being found. From being alone to being united—in holy matrimony.

As Pete and Annie completed their walk of a lifetime, my husband gave our daughter to Tom. The rest of us grinned, almost embarrassed by our voyeurism as we watched Tom admire his bride. The two of them then stepped forward to a blubbering Pastor Scott and committed their lives to each other.

"You'll never walk alone again," was the promise they made to one another.

• • •

After the ceremony, the wedding reception moved to a large ranch east of town that hosted special events. You never know what to expect from the weather in Central Oregon, yet the September sun shone brightly that day.

The invitations had specified the wedding would be an

"alcohol-free celebration" to honor not only Annie and Tom but also their many friends in recovery who would be attending. At the reception we provided a full espresso bar instead of alcohol, and the line for lattes and mochas, hot or iced, was as long as it might have been for mixed drinks.

Midway through dinner, Pete rose to collectively welcome our guests and to offer the first toast.

"It isn't often that I use this word," he began, "but today I feel *blessed*. Blessed to have this gathering of family and friends, many of whom have traveled a long way to celebrate this great day with us. I feel blessed that my wife, Barbara, is still by my side after all these years. I feel blessed that Annie has returned to us and our family is intact again. And I feel blessed to now welcome Tom into our family. Here's to you, Annie and Tom, and to your new life together." We all lifted our champagne flutes, full of sparkling cider, to the bride and groom.

Dinner culminated with an a cappella "toast" from Briana, who sang "The Way You Look Tonight." Once staunch competitors in high school, both in and out of choir, their relationship had since matured into deep affection. Briana had graduated from college at the height of Annie's meth addiction, and Annie could now crack jokes about the different paths they'd taken. "You win, Briana. Hands down—you win!"

The sun grew weary as the celebration wore on, ultimately giving way to a full and luminescent moon. Against the blackened sky, it was the perfect backdrop for the black-and-white wedding, just as if we'd ordered it, and the party continued under twinkling lights. By this time, Pete had his baseball cap back on.

• • •

Not long after the wedding, Annie and I pushed shopping carts side by side through Safeway one afternoon. She was looking for the ingredients for a new concoction she was going to try in the kitchen. Cooking was yet another new territory of exploration for her, much to Tom's relief so he could occasionally hang up the apron he'd never wanted to put on.

Although Annie had once lived on meth, Mountain Dew, and fast food—if she ate at all—that day in the supermarket was just another snapshot of how much had changed. I watched in amazement as she made her healthy selections, plucking organic foods from the shelves and comparing the sugar content of one product over another. Also mindful of price, Annie looked like any other housewife on a mission, that is, if one who still looked sixteen could appear to be a housewife. It was all just so normal. The impossible had somehow become possible. My dream had miraculously become reality.

Annie and I were already giddy, and having more fun than should be allowed with shopping carts, when a familiar song began to play over the public address system. It's always amazed me how Annie knows the lyrics to virtually every song ever written, especially those from the generation before hers. She recognized the song instantly as the processional from her dad's and my wedding, the Graham Nash song that had provided the sentiments as we headed down the aisle and began our life together.

Annie turned to me with that mischievous look of hers, grabbed her cell phone as a stand-in microphone, and began to sing:

> *Our house, is a very, very, very fine house;*
> *With two cats in the yard, life used to be so hard . . .*

Oblivious to the other shoppers, Annie and I danced. We circled each other, rocking to the music and delighting in the moment. It was then that I realized the words to Pete's and my song were truer than they'd ever been.

⤜•⤛

# CHAPTER 30

# My Favorite Felons

Annie and Tom celebrated their first wedding anniversary in Barcelona, Spain—attending the biannual International Narcotics Anonymous convention. The trip was a wedding gift from my brother and Pete's sister.

Before heading home, the still-newlyweds made a detour through Paris. Robin booked them into the same hotel where she and I had stayed more than three years before. It somehow seemed fitting that Annie visit the very sites where I'd found solace during those last days of her active addiction. In fact, my favorite photo of their trip is one of Annie inside Notre-Dame Cathedral. Wearing a simple pink T-shirt and framed by towering stone pillars nearly a millennium old, Annie lit a candle, just as I had done for her high atop the city at Sacré Cœur.

"I lit the candle," she said, "for all of those who still suffer."

• • •

Annie and Tom are fine young adults—"our favorite felons," as Pete likes to call them. They work hard at their jobs, and Annie has just graduated from college with a bachelor's degree in general science, with an emphasis in chemistry. It was on her nickel this time.

Seven years clean, they still make twelve-step meetings a part of their lives, and both take helping the newcomer seriously. Tom has launched the construction business he envisioned the day I first met him, and he gives work to those newly in recovery or freshly out of prison—just as had been done for him. Tom has also reunited with his young son. He's not parenting Isaiah directly, but their relationship is a special one.

While infrequent, Annie's edgy "addict" persona occasionally rears its ugly head—her "evil twin," as I call it. But she most typically exudes serenity and compassion for others. She now takes twelve-step meetings into the county jail where she'd once sat among the incarcerated hopeless. Annie says some will occasionally show up later at a meeting on the outside "because you told me there was hope here." She and Tom have also given refuge in their home to newly clean addicts with nowhere else to go. Their "home for wayward girls," they sometimes muse.

If Annie does nothing else in her lifetime than help show others the way out, she'll forever be my hero. I suspect this is the "greatness" that my friend Virginia had envisioned when she'd prophesized to me that day about Annie's future.

Another way Annie and Tom give back to the community is to tell their stories in our local middle and high schools. Under the umbrella of the Meth Action Coalition here in Central Oregon, Annie, Tom, and others—including Michelle from our early MFFSG meetings—share their stories of addiction and life on the streets. It's a humbling exercise to tell an audience of teenagers about your fall into the abyss, but the kids are listening. Maybe some who are at risk will be saved.

"It's not worth it," Annie tells them. "The drug will always win. Find healthy ways to belong somewhere and to deal with your feelings. There's a better way. If you do what I did, chances are you'll remain there, suffer there, die there. Few make it out."

At one of these presentations in a high school health class, Jeff first heard his sister tell her story. An insightful student asked, "I want to hear from the brother. What was all of this like for you?"

"For the longest time I didn't understand," Jeff answered, "but I think I do now. There's been forgiveness." It was a great day for Annie to have finally made peace with her brother.

Annie and Tom are fortunate to have emerged from meth addiction with their health and all their teeth intact. Annie's had some memory loss, though, and it's unfortunately some of the good stuff. Her tongue ring is now buried somewhere in our catchall kitchen junk drawer, but the tattoo is still evident.

And I am a former smoker once again.

My daughter and I are careful with our boundaries now, and while I sometimes miss the enmeshed closeness we once had, I know what we now have is better for both of us. I still worry about her some but find freedom in my prayers. Much of her life is no longer my business, and that's as it should be.

If Annie hadn't fallen off the cliff of addiction so hard and so fast, and if she hadn't needed to change absolutely everything about her life for her very survival, I wonder if she ever would have. She might still be just another pretty girl with an entitled attitude and a drink in her hand, going from one relationship to the next. Our country seems to be full of those girls right now, many of whom adorn the magazine covers that line our grocery store checkout lanes.

"I'm not that girl anymore," Annie says. "I'll never be that girl again."

Annie and Tom are fiercely committed to one another, but that's not to say there's anything perfect about their relationship. Their lives are a miracle, not a fairy tale. They've had their struggles, as all couples do, and their occasional blowouts undoubtedly rattle the windows in their respectable Bend neighborhood. But they're as playful as they are intense. They "get" each other. There's an uncommon connectedness between them that not all couples share, and they have the wisdom of their program to help them over the hurdles.

While on the surface Annie and Tom's lives look fully "normal," upon closer inspection some underlying dysfunction is

A Very Fine House

evident. In a marriage where both partners are recovering meth addicts, reformed smokers, caffeine junkies, gym rats, and night owls—not to mention both of whom are racked with a truckload of ADHD—theirs is a chaotic household.

Annie says cheerfully, "If it wasn't for the last minute, nothing would ever get done."

It's a daily occurrence for Tom to misplace his cell phone, wallet, or truck keys—if not all three at once. Last Fourth of July he did just that when all three were unwittingly locked in his truck ... along with both dogs. Chaotic indeed.

A fun scene from the movie *Superman* charmingly illustrates Annie and Tom's fragile interdependence, their perfect imperfection. In it Superman (Christopher Reeve) swoops through the sky at the speed of sound to catch Lois Lane, just in the nick of time, as she free-falls from a crippled helicopter sitting atop a skyscraper. As he masterfully catches her in midair, with every perfect hair still impeccably in place, Superman victoriously declares, "Don't worry, miss, I've got you." To this Lois replies, "Yes, but who's got *you*?"

It's my unprofessional opinion that Annie has never had bipolar disorder, II or otherwise. Her brain is a puzzle, for sure, and her temperament still reactive and easily overwhelmed. But it's clear to me that the "craziness" that once manifested was alcohol and drug induced. Those were facts she always omitted in her many consultations with mental health professionals. The tool kit of recovery and the support of a loving husband seem to be the only medicine she needs these days. This is not the solution for everyone, however. Many addicts have significant co-occurring disorders that require close medical supervision and carefully prescribed medications. Recovery from drugs will prove nearly impossible for some if the addiction and other mental health issues are not treated concurrently.

The "poor coping skills" diagnosis offered by the psychiatrist in Phoenix sure seems an understatement for one who suffered so much. Whatever the reason, the lessons Annie needed to learn

-246-

weren't ones I was able to teach her—hard as I did try. I'm just so grateful there are others like her who are doing the job.

My journey with Annie through her addiction has changed me in almost every way. My faith is deeper and more authentic, and my judgments fewer. I thought I knew what an addict looked like, but as with most things we judge, I've discovered there is no stereotype. Addiction can befall anyone. I've also found that it's not my job to figure out Annie's life—or anyone else's, for that matter. I don't have to change anyone. Letting people be who they are frees us all, and my only job is to become the person I wish others to be.

My politics have shifted from right to left. As much as I would like to, no longer do I believe that every man and woman in America has an equal chance—we simply aren't born with equal brains. Not all people can pull themselves up by their proverbial bootstraps, because, as my friend Christi says, "We haven't all been issued the same boots." Some of us need more help than others. I've learned that while no one chooses addiction, they *can* choose recovery—hard as that may be. And I've come to realize that (almost) no one should forever be defined by his or her worst act. Change your choices; change your life.

I even decorate my house differently now. Gone is the country theme, as if that was some sort of prescription for happily ever after.

• • •

It's been a few years since Pete and I downsized out of the big house in which we raised Jeff and Annie. With both of them now grown and on their own, Pete and I were ready for a new space and a chance to reinvent ourselves as a couple.

Shortly before the movers came, the four of us rendezvoused on the family room floor over a Thanksgiving weekend and shared a Taco Bell dinner, just like we'd done twenty years before on the day we moved into the house. We spent hours hashing over old stories and treasured memories, and prepared to let go of that phase of our lives as we moved forward into the next. It was bittersweet.

Given Bend's wicked postrecession housing market, I often refer to the sale of that house as the second miracle of our lives. The deal came together quickly, and with just thirty days to find another home and move, we had to act quickly. I put the word out to my church fellowship through a broadcast email, asking for help with packing and moving excess furniture into storage. Having repeatedly cooked and packed for others, I felt certain there were redeemable coupons at my disposal, yet only one person responded to my request. What happened instead on that day was that Annie and Tom, along with four men from recovery whom we'd never met, showed up with three trucks in thirteen-degree weather, pushing through eight inches of newly fallen snow.

I'm not exactly sure what the lesson was that day, but it certainly seemed ironic that it was the addicts who helped when the church did not.

"That's what we do, Mom," Annie said. "We show up for each other."

I sometimes think the recovery community is a picture of what the church should look like. I've experienced the Spirit of God hovering in those recovery rooms as a palpable presence, bringing healing to those who struggle and who submit to their higher power. It's my belief that Jesus, my Higher Power, hears those prayers, whether or not they know his name. His favorite people were, after all, the most broken among us—the outcasts, the misfits, the sick, and, yes, the addicts.

Several days after moving into our new home, I fetched our dog, Delores, from the yard and encountered our new neighbor, John. It was December. John, a snowbird, was in town for just the night. We exchanged pleasantries and shared email addresses. When a follow-up email from him arrived the next week, I was struck by the tagline at the bottom of his message: www.not alone.org. It was familiar somehow. When I checked the website, I instantly recognized the book featured on the home page. Dr.

John Vawter was a pastor with a daughter recovering from heroin addiction, and his book, *Hit by a Ton of Bricks: You're Not Alone When Your Child's on Drugs,* had been in my reading arsenal when Annie was on the streets years before.

I could only wonder, *What was God up to now?*

• • •

All I'd wanted was for my daughter to stop killing herself with drugs, and I'd never considered that recovery is about so much more than abstinence. It's a whole new way of life and an entirely new way of thinking. Annie is a new woman, more whole and complete than I ever could have imagined. She has finally shown up for her life, claiming it as her own. It's as if she's awakened from years of troubled slumber and can now talk about her bad dreams. She's acquired wisdom uncommon in someone her age, if at any age, and I couldn't be prouder of her than if she'd just dismantled a doomsday bomb to save the human race.

I can hardly wrap my mind around the magnificence of what has occurred in my life. I don't know why Annie was saved from almost certain death when there are so many who are lost and suffering. Or why our family was restored to wholeness when so many parents grieve. I'd tried to prepare myself for a different outcome, the one I felt more likely, but now receive this immense gift with humility, gratitude, and awe.

Every time I see Annie's pretty face or take in the fragrance of her perfect cheek as I kiss it, it's like reopening the gift all over again. All I can do is prayerfully whisper my thanks.

I'd asked God to free Annie but didn't know what that might look like. I thought it possible her freedom might come in heaven. That's the way it happens for many, for God-only-knows reasons.

Annie offers her explanation. "All I know," she says, "is that someone, or something, greater than I am delivered me from the hell that was my life."

Many people in our lives have made the mistaken assumption that Pete's and my efforts are responsible for Annie's success in recovery, when nothing could be further from the truth. The irony is that I'd been trying to *will* Annie into doing things for years, and when the stakes were at their highest, I became the most helpless. Our only chance of getting our daughter back was to, paradoxically, let her go.

Although we lived and breathed a single-minded determination to advocate for her whenever an opportunity presented itself, Annie is clean today because of what *she's* done, and what God has done in her. We merely supported her recovery and stood by her while she saved herself. The treatment we paid for was only as effective as Annie's willingness to change. She does the hard work, which no one can do for her, and it's a choice she makes every day — if not multiple times a day. Pete and I are merely grateful bystanders to the miracle that has changed not only our daughter, but us as well.

While Annie and Tom are always on guard to protect the anonymity of those in their program, I occasionally hear them make reference to someone "going out." This is slang for relapse. The knowledge that this could happen to them is a fear I carry. I wish I could say I feel stronger for what I've already survived, but the truth is that in some ways I feel more vulnerable. Gone is denial, and I live with full knowledge of what's possible. The statistics for drug addicts remaining in long-term recovery aren't great. For some, relapse can be a weekend; for others, a lifetime — if they survive it at all. As Tom told me, the disease is progressive even when an addict isn't using, so the symptoms of relapse can look even worse than the disease as it previously manifested.

I'm impressed that Annie and Tom have a relapse plan to protect themselves should one or the other ever pick up again. The deeper each of them moves into recovery, the less likely this potential seems, but it's not unheard-of that people with ten years, twenty years clean, or more, will toss in the recovery towel. Addicts do, after all, have a lifelong disease.

The final chapters of Annie and Tom's lives have not yet been written, but one thing is clear: whatever the future holds for them, it is not up to me.

Learning that we can't save our children, whether or not they are addicts, is the saddest lesson of my life. Choosing to survive my daughter when she was in active addiction — choosing to cross over to safety — is the scariest thing I've ever done. But for those who grieve what their children have become, or may never become, there is an unexpected gift. Who knew we could save ourselves?

• • •

Mine is the story of the proverbial prodigal son, or daughter, and Annie returned to us, having squandered everything we'd ever given her. She was lost, but now she's found. A life resurrected and indeed freed from bondage — if maybe just for today.

Our family has by no means been reframed as another Norman Rockwell painting. Our story now includes addiction. It's a part of who we are, and, in an odd sort of way, I'm proud of it. Norman doesn't live here anymore, and we really don't want him back. We're more authentic now. We've cast a broader net into the world. I don't want to even venture a guess as to what kind of painting we might look like now, but whatever it is, it's eclectic, edgy, alive, and real.

• • •

On the last weekend of summer, I sat at my desk, putting the finishing touches on these pages, when I heard several loud toots of a horn outside. From my kitchen window I saw Annie roll in to our driveway. With her head cocked slightly sideways and peering forward through the shimmering windshield, she looked like she'd captured a canary behind her pursed lips, and her eyes twinkled with a look-what-I've-done-now naughtiness. There she sat, perched inside a flawless new Camry — a black one.

The transmission had just died in her very used car the day

before, and after a full day of kicking tires at every dealership in Bend, she and Tom settled on the Camry. I guess it just had to be.

Annie came around to open the passenger side with an invitation for me to jump in. The grief I'd felt years before came rushing to the surface. My daughter and I locked moist eyes in mutual recognition of this crowning allegory of restoration. "Yeah, I know," she said. "Kind of poetic, isn't it?"

# Postscript

Addiction is shamefully undertreated in the United States. Only one in ten addicts reports receiving any treatment at all. Nearly a quarter of all deaths each year are attributable to tobacco, alcohol, and other drugs.

There are presently 2.3 million Americans incarcerated in our prisons. That's the highest number per capita in the world. Depending on the source cited, it's estimated that at least half of these inmates, and likely many more, meet the medical criteria for substance addiction. Dr. McCauley told us it's time to treat addiction as the public health catastrophe it's become.

Staying clean may be the hardest part of recovery for those who do find help, but reentry is nearly as difficult. Our system punishes addicts for the rest of their lives. For most, drug addiction ultimately becomes synonymous with criminality, and a criminal record follows them everywhere and forever. In my town, every rental agency has a bold notation on the application telling convicted felons not to apply. Those applicants will be rejected without exception, regardless of the time that's elapsed. Nearly every employment application in this country asks about criminal convictions, and many professions expressly deny licensure or certification to felons. After seven years clean, Tom was denied a life insurance policy.

One can't leave their addiction without a better place to go. Without a job or a decent place to live, the most fundamental of needs, only the most industrious and the most diligent seem able to make it. In Annie's case, I believe part of what motivated her to seek recovery was that she ultimately valued her family over drugs. But many addicts have burned their bridges home, losing not just critical support but motivation to even get clean. Many of the sick and lost go back through the revolving doors of our prison system, the bulging human warehouses where the victims of this disease are treated largely by wardens rather than doctors.

Addicts seem forever branded as "less than." For those who do recover, when do we forgive? How long is long enough? When do we as a society allow a person who has done the hard work to reclaim their place beside us, without discrimination and without judgment?

Annie told me recently that on one particularly dark day on the streets, she reached out with a phone call to an old friend from high school. The girl had been a longtime friend and was the best Christian she knew. Annie found the streets of Bend a godless place, and feeling spiritually bankrupt, she groped for a lifeline. Surely this girl would throw her one.

When Annie connected with her on the phone, the friend's message was simple: "God is punishing you."

Really? God was punishing Annie? This was the Christian message a friend had for her? Where is the hope in that? And if it's true, why would God do such a thing?

Did Annie need to be punished because of some inherent "badness" in her that needed correcting? Was Annie guilty because she succumbed to substances just to feel normal? Or was she being punished for that one, very human, reckless moment when her life changed forever, the moment when she accepted a line of cocaine but it turned out to be meth? Was the ensuing addiction, homelessness, criminality, and self-loathing a punishment from God?

*What would Annie want with a God like that?*

And what of our family's suffering? Were we being punished as well?

Upon hearing this, I was again grateful for the little church that had supported me so completely during the most difficult time of my life, and that had also embraced my troubled daughter. Annie needed *release* from her shame, not more of it. In our little community of God-lovers, there was the understanding that we are all in various states of brokenness ourselves; it's just more apparent in some of us than in others.

I know Annie's friend meant her no harm, and that she was simply sharing the message she'd been taught. Many of us have been taught to judge those whose lives look different from ours. Some want to simplify the messiness of life by tying up all their rules into one neat little box. But I don't think that's where God lives—he's far too big for that. In fact, I believe Jesus came to let us out of the box.

The judgment of others can also come from sheer ignorance. I can see why Annie's friend may have looked at her with disdain, believing she'd brought God's wrath on herself. Most people do look at drug addicts in moral terms. "It's your own fault," they'll say. "Drugs are bad, and you shouldn't have done what you did." If my own kid hadn't become a drug addict, I might not get it either. Some close to me still don't.

Shortly after Annie came home from treatment, my therapist initiated a women's support group, of which I'm still a part, and we often talk about this very thing. All six of us have adult children who have had serious issues, running the gamut of various mental illnesses, disorders, and addictions—all of whom have been deemed gifted at some time in their lives. "Nutty kids," as I call them.

In our group we regularly observe with amusement the parents who feign perfection in their homes, concealing the warts we all wear. Even if their seemingly obedient, compliant, accomplished, *perfect* children are indeed that, those parents often take full credit

for having reared them to be that way. And why shouldn't they—
they don't know the difference. But we who have raised challenging children know the truth. We know the playing field is not a
level one.

Good parenting is, without question, the most critical ingredi-
ent in raising healthy and capable children, but if there's anything
I've learned, it in no way guarantees the results. I know wonderful
mothers and fathers, in otherwise high-functioning families, who
have a child, or children, who for one reason or another cannot
"do life" well. There is so much in the genetic mix that contrib-
utes to this that has nothing to do with parenting.

I liken one's luck with offspring to Forrest Gump's proverbial box of chocolates—"You never know what you're gonna
get." Some of us get mouthwatering milk chocolate truffles with
delightfully succulent centers, a bite of which sends us into a near
coma of contentment. On the other hand, many get bittersweet
chocolate-covered nuts, where the salt alone can totally suck a
parent dry.

Whether or not we are addicts, we are all just one bad decision
away from disaster. A reckless moment, a careless act, can change
the course of our lives forever. Life can happen in an instant, and
the consequences can be devastating and far-reaching. But is that
something God does to us?

Those who might judge the disasters of others may not yet
have had their own.

These past years I've listened to scores of recovering addicts
tell their stories. Not one of them reports a day in which they
awakened and said to themselves, "Ya know, today I'm gonna go
out into the world and totally screw up my life." All had hopes
and dreams for their futures, and not one of them saw addiction
in it. It may have begun as a spontaneous act on the school bus,
a trip to their parents' medicine cabinet, drinks at a frat party, or
a snort behind the garage. Many tell a seemingly benign story of
first use. They believed their experimentation to be harmless, but
what followed was one boundary violation after another. Friends

are doing it; sometimes even parents are doing it. And if one is wired for addiction, continued use may become necessary just to feel normal.

Many of Annie's friends in recovery report having been raised by addicts or by otherwise dysfunctional or abusive parents. They struggle in recovery because they haven't a clue what "normal" even looks like. Just as many of them, however, had at least one attentive parent and came from loving environments. Some were even raised in homes that were alcohol free.

It's been my observation that most of them, like Annie, share the common feeling, *I wasn't enough*. They weren't pretty enough, cool enough, smart enough, thin enough, strong enough, tall enough, tough enough, clever enough. "I didn't know where I belonged," many have said. So for some addicts, initial drug use is an attempt to fit in somewhere, anywhere. The "nutty" ones do have an uncanny ability to find one another, and drugs can provide a commonality that binds them together. It actually works for a while—right up until the time it ruins their lives.

Addicts aren't unique in having the feeling of "I'm not enough." It's a hallmark of the middle school and high school years, and I remember feeling it too. Those who feel it the most, like Annie, are often overly sensitive and emotionally fragile, and they may suffer from any number of disorders such as ADHD, depression, or anxiety. Or they can be somewhere on the continuum of mood disorders. Annie says her drug use was more about trying to feel normal than about getting high.

My good friend Nancy tells me she can no longer look at a lone, darkened silhouette with a backpack in quite the same way anymore. The telltale sign of a street addict, this obscure, shuffling figure—head down and face shadowed by the hood of a jacket or sweatshirt—Nancy now knows, is a sick and suffering human being. It's someone's son or daughter, and somewhere someone grieves for them.

That faceless shadow was once my daughter. It was Tom. It was Archie, Mike, and Michelle, and the many other addicts I have come to know and love. I send up prayers that those who still suffer will find recovery, and I pray for peace for the many who will not.

Not all addicts live on the street, though. In fact, most do not. Whether it's alcohol, marijuana, pills, or the "white stuff"—or any number of compulsive behaviors—addicts are everywhere. They're where we work, play, worship, and go to school. Addiction does not discriminate. It knows no color, no ethnicity, no religion, no gender or sexual orientation. It affects the young and the old, the rich and the poor, the famous and the invisible, the brilliant and the not so very brilliant. It doesn't know one side of the tracks from the other. Addicts live in our neighborhoods, next door, in the bedroom down the hall—and they sometimes sleep beside us.

My new friend Archie was once deemed a career criminal by our local law enforcement. With fifty-seven arrests and five prison terms, he spent nine of the fifteen years of his active addiction behind bars. Yet he is now a model citizen, college student, youth addiction counselor, and prison liaison, giving back to the community from which he'd taken so much. He quips, "I even have a debit card now, and with *my* name on it."

Archie's wedding was one for the record books. He married a probation officer. The police officer who nearly shot him during a foot chase years ago stood up for him as his best man. Such is the miracle of recovery.

When Archie tells his story, he'll often say, "I don't know if I was born an addict, or if an addict was born the day I first tried drugs." I believe that question has now been answered. In August 2011, the American Society of Addiction Medicine (ASAM) released a new definition of addiction in an eight-page statement that supports many of the things Dr. McCauley had taught us at Family Week. It was the result of a four-year process involving more than eighty leading experts in addiction and neurology.

In its August 15, 2011, report on the new definition of addiction, NBCNews.com quoted one of the overseers of the study:

"At its core, addiction isn't just a social problem or moral problem or criminal problem. It's a brain problem whose behaviors manifest in all these other areas," said Dr. Michael Miller, past president of ASAM who oversaw the development of the new definition. "Many behaviors driven by addiction are real problems and sometimes criminal acts. But the disease is about the brain, not drugs. It's about underlying neurology, not outward actions."*

The website also quoted Dr. Miller as saying, "We have to stop moralizing, blaming, controlling or smirking at the person with the disease of addiction, and start creating opportunities for individuals and families to get help …"

NBCNews.com further reported, "The new definition also describes addiction as a primary disease, meaning that it's not the result of other causes, such as emotional or psychiatric problems. And like cardiovascular disease and diabetes, addiction is recognized as a chronic disease; so it must be treated, managed and monitored over a person's lifetime, the researchers say."

The chicken-or-egg question that has confounded Archie, and certainly this mother as well, about what came first—the neurological disorder or the compulsive behaviors and substance use—was answered by Dr. Raju Hajela, chair of the ASAM committee that formulated addiction's new definition. "The disease creates distortions in thinking, feelings and perceptions, which drive people to behave in ways that are not understandable to others around them … Simply put, addiction is not a choice. *Addictive behaviors are a manifestation of the disease, not a cause*" (emphasis added).

Voila.

This news came on the heels of the American Board of Addiction Medicine's (ABAM) announcement a month earlier that ten

---

* "Addiction Now Defined as Brain Disorder, Not Behavior Issue," NBCNews.com, www.nbcnews.com/id/44147493/ns/health-addictions/t/addiction-now-defined-brain-disorder-not-behavior-issue/ (accessed February 12, 2014).

new addiction residency programs had just been launched across the country, with more to follow. Heretofore, physicians have received virtually no training in addiction, and the prescribing behaviors of some actually serve to enable it. But there will now be more residency-trained addiction specialists, just as there are in others specialties such as oncology (cancer), nephrology (kidney), and cardiology (heart). Finally, addicts will have more comprehensive care at their disposal as the patients that they are.

I've heard experts forecast that huge leaps will be made in the field of addiction in the next ten to twenty years. It makes me wonder if addiction will always be a medical problem with a spiritual solution, or if medical advancements will bring a curative pill or genetic solutions. While one doesn't choose addiction, in his ABAM statement Dr. Hajela points out that choice plays a role in getting help. "Because there is no pill which alone can cure addiction, choosing recovery over unhealthy behaviors is necessary."

Dr. McCauley was right. This is indeed information "with power to change the world."

# Gifts

- ➻ Get out of the way.
- ➻ No one stays in addiction without help.
- ➻ Don't do for another what they can do for themselves.
- ➻ Don't pick up the rope.
- ➻ If nothing changes, then nothing changes.★
- ➻ It's not your fault.
- ➻ Allow natural consequences.
- ➻ Get support.
- ➻ Let go and let God.
- ➻ Our secrets make us sick.
- ➻ It's not up to me.
- ➻ Act, not react.
- ➻ Choose joy.
- ➻ Raise the bottom through intervention, if possible.
- ➻ 25/25/25.
- ➻ Practice gratitude.

---

★ This principle is attributed to C. P. Sennett.

→ Get on with your own life.

→ Take care of yourself.

→ Don't push the river.

→ Wait for the miracle.

→ Just for today.

→ Be the person you wish others to be.

→ Pray, pray, pray.

> *God, grant me the serenity*
> *to accept the things I cannot change;*
> *courage to change the things I can;*
> *and wisdom to know the difference.*

# Acknowledgments

I would first like to thank Annie for graciously allowing me to so openly share the very personal details of her life. She allowed me to do so with the hope that other families like ours, and other addicts like her, might be helped as they struggle with this devastating disease. You're so brave, Annie.

Thank you also to Tom for telling me to "hold nothing back." You're the son-in-law I'd prayed for, and I couldn't love you more.

To Jeff, who lights up my life, thank you for being the wonderful man you've become, and are still becoming. If you ever do drugs, I will beat you senseless.

To my dear Pete, who usually lets me have my own way, thank you for all the nights you spent alone while I wrote. I should be free again on our next anniversary, and we can dance to our song.

To Paul, who first encouraged me in this endeavor, I thank you for your immense support and feedback. Had you not been so kind with your initial feedback, I may never have kept writing.

To James Lund, whom I approached as a novice writer looking for expert editorial help, your guidance and instruction made all the difference. I could not have done this without you.

To my neighbor, Dr. John Vawter—my question about our fateful meeting has at least been partially answered. Thank you for referring me to James Lund.

To Alice Crider, my agent at WordServe Literary, thank you for believing in my story and for taking a chance with me. You're another miracle in my life.

To John Sloan, my editor, thank you for embracing my story so quickly, and for turning the ship around! To Londa Alderink, Dirk Buursma, and all of the other fine people at Zondervan, thank you for your work to make this book a reality.

To Amy Belasen, thank you for your class.

To Dr. Kevin McCauley, your teaching helped me to forgive. Thank you for allowing me to quote you so extensively (www. instituteforaddictionstudy.com).

To the treatment professionals who helped Annie in both Oregon and California, thank you for showing her there's a way out.

To Karen, and to the ladies of our first Wednesday group, thank you for being the "flowers in our amazing bouquet of support." Some of your wisdom I've shared in this book.

To Scott and Kari and our CCC church family, thank you for your safe and warm embrace. The recession may have claimed our little church, but not what we shared together.

To the families of MFFSG, thank you for sharing your lives, your stories, and your sorrows. Don't think I would have made it through without you.

To those I've served with on the Meth Action Coalition, thank you for your vision and commitment to this community-wide drug prevention effort.

To the men and women of the Bend Police Department and the Deschutes County Sheriff's Office, Adult Parole and Probation, district attorney's office, and the judges of the Circuit Court, thank you for the hard work you do. Without exception, every individual we dealt with in our county's legal system was kind, respectful, helpful, and compassionate.

To all of the addicts I've known and loved, both here and now gone, thank you for blessing me with your lives and your courage.

And to His Most High—*thank you, thank you, thank you.*

# Resources

## WEBSITES TO FIND TWELVE-STEP MEETINGS AND INFORMATION ON RECOVERY

**Al-Anon and Alateen**
www.al-anon.org
www.al-anon.alateen.org

**Nar-Anon**
www.nar-anon.org

**Narcotics Anonymous**
www.na.org

**Alcoholics Anonymous**
www.alcoholics-anonymous.org

**Celebrate Recovery**
www.celebraterecovery.com

**National Alliance on Mental Illness**
www.nami.org

## OTHER INFORMATIVE WEBSITES

**American Society of Addiction Medicine**
www.asam.org

**Substance Abuse and Mental Health Services Administration (SAMHSA)**
www.samhsa.gov
NOTE: There is a wonderful treatment locator tool on this site.

**National Institute on Drug Abuse**
www.drugabuse.gov

**The Institute for Addiction Study (Dr. Kevin McCauley)**
www.instituteforaddictionstudy.com

**Love First**
www.lovefirst.net

**Community Anti-Drug Coalitions of America (CADCA)**
www.cadca.org

**Meth Action Coalition**
www.methaction.org

**Parent Pathway: Supporting Your Journey Through a Child's Addiction**
www.parentpathway.com

**Lighthouse Network**
www.notalone.org

**Hazelden**
www.hazelden.org

**Partnership for a Drug-Free America**
www.drugfree.org

**Oxford Houses**
www.oxfordhouse.org

## Books I Found Helpful

Anonymous. *One Day at a Time in Al-Anon.* Virginia Beach, VA: Al-Anon Family Group Headquarters, 1968, 1972, 1973.

———. *Courage to Change: One Day at a Time in Al-Anon II.* Virginia Beach, VA: Al-Anon Family Group Headquarters, 1968, 1972, 1973.

Beattie, Melody. *Codependent No More: How to Stop Controlling Others and Start Caring for Yourself.* Center City, MN: Hazelden, 1986, 1992.

*The Bible.*

Fontaine, Claire and Mia Fontaine. *Come Back: A Mother and Daughter's Journey through Hell and Back.* New York: HarperCollins, 2006.

Jay, Debra. *No More Letting Go: The Spirituality of Taking Action Against Alcoholism and Drug Addiction.* New York: Bantam, 2006.

Jay, Jeff, and Debra Jay. *Love First: A Family's Guide to Intervention.* Center City, MN: Hazelden, 2000, 2008.

Lamott, Anne. *Traveling Mercies: Some Thoughts on Faith.* New York: Anchor, 2000.

Lawford, Christopher Kennedy. *Symptoms of Withdrawal: A Memoir of Snapshots and Redemption.* New York: HarperCollins, 2005.

Rubin, Charles. *Don't Let Your Kids Kill You: A Guide for Parents of Drug and Alcohol Addicted Children.* Rockport, MA: Element, 1996.

Sheff, David. *Beautiful Boy: A Father's Journey Through His Son's Addiction.* New York: Mariner, 2007.

Vawter, John. *Hit by a Ton of Bricks: You're Not Alone When Your Child's on Drugs*. Little Rock, AK: Family Life, 2003.

Waterston, Ellen. *Then There Was No Mountain: The Parallel Odyssey of a Mother and Daughter through Addiction*. Lanham, MD: Taylor, 2003.

Wandzilak, Kristina, and Constance Curry. *The Lost Years: Surviving a Mother and Daughter's Worst Nightmare*. Santa Monica, CA: Jeffers, 2006.